always up to date

The law changes, but Nolo is on top of it! We offer several ways to make sure you and your Nolo products are up to date:

1 **Nolo's Legal Updater**
We'll send you an email whenever a new edition of this book is published! Sign up at **www.nolo.com/legalupdater**.

2 **Updates @ Nolo.com**
Check **www.nolo.com/update** to find recent changes in the law that affect the current edition of your book.

3 **Nolo Customer Service**
To make sure that this edition of the book is the most recent one, call us at **800-728-3555** and ask one of our friendly customer service representatives. Or find out at **www.nolo.com**.

please note

We believe accurate, plain-English legal information should help you solve many of your own legal problems. But this text is not a substitute for personalized advice from a knowledgeable lawyer. If you want the help of a trained professional—and we'll always point out situations in which we think that's a good idea—consult an attorney licensed to practice in your state.

2nd edition

The Performance Appraisal Handbook

Legal & Practical Rules for Managers

by Amy DelPo

SECOND EDITION   MARCH 2007

Editor   LISA GUERIN

Cover Design   SUSAN PUTNEY

Book Design   TERRI HEARSH

Production   MARGARET LIVINGSTON

Index   JEAN MANN

Proofreading   JOE SADUSKY

Printing   CONSOLIDATED PRINTERS, INC

DelPo, Amy, 1967-
    The performance appraisal handbook : legal & practical rules for managers/
    by Amy DelPo.-- 2nd ed.
        p. cm.
      Contents: An overview of performance appraisal -- Legal traps -- Performance
    objectives -- Observation and documentation -- The interim meeting -- The year-end
    performance appraisal -- Progressive discipline.
    ISBN-13: 978-1-4133-0567-8
    ISBN-10: 1-4133-0567-8
      1. Employees--Rating of--United States. 2. Employees--Rating of--Law and
    legislation--United States--Popular works. I. Title.

    HF5549.5.R3D44 2007
    658.3'125--dc22

                                                            2006047150

Quantity sales: For information on bulk purchases or corporate premium
sales, please contact the Special Sales Department. For academic sales or
textbook adoptions, ask for Academic Sales. Call 800-955-4775 or write to
Nolo, 950 Parker Street, Berkeley, CA 94710.

Acknowledgments

I would like to thank the following people who helped make this book possible:

My wonderful editor on the first edition of this book, Stephanie Bornstein, whose legal experience, hard work, and attention to detail made the finished book worlds better than the draft I handed her at the beginning of the process. More important, her sense of humor and constant support kept me sane.

Thanks also to my editor on the second edition, Lisa Guerin, for being her usual efficient, professional, and easy-going self. I've been writing and editing books with Lisa since 2001, and it's always a pleasure.

MindSolve's Dan Boccabella and Jeff Lyons, who came to Nolo and me searching for a way to serve their customers even better. Their desire to provide the best and most complete information to MindSolve users was the inspiration for this book, and their input has helped make it an invaluable tool for frontline managers everywhere.

Nolo's Sigrid Metson, whose enthusiasm for this project never waned, even when mine did. Without her vision and business savvy, this book never would have seen the light of day. Anyone with so much energy and so many ideas is surely a national treasure.

The members of the advisory board: Harold Fethe, Ellen Lopresti, Greg Lynn, Jeff Lyons, Margie Mader-Clark, and Sigrid Metson. I cannot thank them enough for their insightful comments and valuable suggestions on the first edition of this book. They generously gave me the benefit of their human resources and management experience to make a strong book even stronger. They are leaders in their fields, and I am honored to have gotten the chance to work with them.

To Margie Mader-Clark, a crackerjack human resources expert, a grateful thanks for adding her voice, and thoughts, to the CD-ROM at the back of this book. And speaking of the CD, thanks to Rich Stim for his expertise and skill in putting it all together for me.

Researcher Stan Jacobson, who haunted countless libraries searching out every book and article that I requested—and who did it all with a smile.

Proofreader Susan Carlson Greene, whose careful eyes kept many errors out of the finished product.

Susan Putney for a wonderful cover design. She had the unenviable task of taking my vague ideas and turning them into something real—and terrific.

Terri Hearsh for designing the book.

And—finally—I'd like to dedicate this book to my son, Charlie, who was born just before I started work on this project. His smile lights up the world.

About the Author

Attorney Amy DelPo brings more than six years of criminal and civil litigation experience to her work at Nolo, having litigated cases in all levels of state and federal courts, including the California Supreme Court and the U.S. Supreme Court. Before joining Nolo's staff in January 2000, DelPo specialized in employment law, handling a wide variety of disputes between employers and employees, including sexual harassment, discrimination, and wage-and-hour issues. DelPo has written and edited numerous employoment law titles for Nolo, including *Dealing With Problem Employees* (coauthor) and *Create Your Own Employee Handbook* (coauthor). DelPo received her law degree with honors from the University of North Carolina at Chapel Hill. She lives in Denver, Colorado, with her husband and two children.

About the Advisory Board

Harold Fethe

Harold Fethe served as Senior Vice President at ALZA Corporation, a leading provider of drug delivery technologies, located in Silicon Valley. In his 30 years at ALZA, Mr. Fethe managed more than 20 annual performance appraisal cycles that produced more than 30,000 individual reviews. During this time, the company's employment counsel rated the company "best managed" among its many Bay Area clients. Mr. Fethe also helped develop and patent an online user interface for performance feedback, which formed the basis for MindSolve Technologies, an entrepreneurial performance management company now in its eighth year of double-digit growth.

Ellen Lopresti

Ellen Lopresti is the director of executive performance management for Capgemini (formerly Ernst & Young), one of the world's leading providers of consulting, technology, and outsourcing services. In her 12 years with the company, she has been the driving force behind the design and implementation of highly effective performance management processes affecting thousands of employees, with a focus on identifying and developing high-potential leaders. Ms. Lopresti also worked as a human resources consultant for both the U.S. Department of Health and Human Services and the Hay Group. She holds a master's degree in industrial/organizational psychology from the University of Baltimore and a bachelor's degree in psychology and business from Ithaca College.

Greg Lynn

Greg Lynn serves as the manager of performance management for JEA in Jacksonville, Florida, one of the largest municipal utilities in the United States. In his 25 years with JEA, Mr. Lynn has held a variety of strategic positions, including director of employee and organizational development, director of training and safety, and manager of quality control. He has worked to develop systems to empower employees and measure performance feedback and reward structures. Mr. Lynn holds a bachelor's degree in industrial management from the Georgia Institute of Technology.

Jeff Lyons

Jeff Lyons in one of the founding principals of MindSolve Technologies and codesigner of MindSolve's industry-leading software suite, MindSolve Visual Performance™ (MVP). Mr. Lyons serves as the company's Chief Client Officer (CCO)—the "buck-stops-here" point person for MindSolve's customers and a key facilitator and adviser from the earliest stages of client relationships. In his 10 years of experience with enterprise-level performance systems, Mr. Lyons has consulted in the design, implementation, and administration of online performance assessment and development processes for a diverse, worldwide client base, including Pfizer, Schroder Investment Management, Sonoco Products, and Capgemini.

Margie Mader-Clark

Margie Mader-Clark has spent more than 16 years in the field of human resources, during which she has held executive and senior management positions in numerous national and global enterprises, including Vontu, Hyperion Solutions, myplay (BMG Records), America OnLine, Netscape Communications, DataFlex, and Network Equipment Technologies. Ms. Mader-Clark has served as a consultant for start-up and midsized companies, specializing in organizational effectiveness, change initiatives, and leadership coaching. She is the author of Nolo's *The Job Description Handbook*. In addition, she serves on the board of the international charity Gifts-in-Kind, Inc.

Sigrid Metson

Sigrid Metson has held senior management positions at leading publishers including Nolo, West, Bancroft-Whitney (the Thomson Corporation), CareThere, and Reference Software. With expertise in building high-performance teams and process reengineering, she has introduced more than 30 information-based products to market. Ms. Metson also played leadership roles in the acquisitions and integrations of Legal Solutions, The Rutter Group, Barclay's, and West Publishing. In addition, she has edited several titles herself, including *Secrets of Successful Writing* (RSI).

Craig Vick

Craig Vick has worked in the field of human resources for 14 years, during which he held executive positions at Owens and Minor Medical, Inc. and Chowan

College, where he also served as adjunct faculty. Mr. Vick's expertise includes training and employee development, preventive labor relations, strategic planning, and performance management. He has also served on the boards of the Urban League of Greater Richmond and the National Industry Liaison Group, and currently serves as the board chairperson of the Richmond Industry Liaison Group. Mr. Vick holds both a master's degree in education and a bachelor's degree in business administration from East Carolina University.

Table of Contents

B Tear-Out Checklists and Forms

Checklists:

Avoiding Legal Trouble

Identifying Job Requirements

Preparing an Employee for Goal Setting

Identifying Goals

Writing Performance Objectives

Documenting Performance

Information to Gather for a Performance Appraisal

Assessing Performance

Common Performance Appraisal Errors

Agenda for the Year-End Appraisal Meeting

Forms:

Performance Log

Kudos to You

Tickler for You

Performance Evaluation

C State and Federal Laws Prohibiting Discrimination

Index

Introduction

I f you are like most managers, conducting performance evaluations is a regular part of your job. All too often, however, managers are told to do performance evaluations without receiving guidance on how to do them well. This book fills that void, providing you with the information and tools you need to make your company's performance appraisal process worthwhile, effective, and even pleasant for your staff and you. This book also does something that is all too rare in a how-to book for managers: It educates you about employment law so that you can avoid legal trouble for your company and yourself while using your legal knowledge to manage your workforce more effectively.

This book provides you with the most cutting edge techniques for conducting effective performance reviews. Using the guidelines presented here will ensure that you continuously improve the performance of your staff and your department each and every day. Indeed, there's no better way to keep your team performing at its peak—and to keep your company at the top of its game.

The Value of Performance Evaluations

If you've been told to conduct performance evaluations, it's because the people who run your company realize that a performance evaluation system can deliver important benefits and improve the success of each employee, each department, and, ultimately, your entire company. And, it's no wonder why. If done properly, performance appraisals can:

- motivate employees to perform better and produce more
- help you identify development and training needs
- help employees understand how they can develop and grow
- increase employee morale
- improve the respect employees have for their managers and senior management
- foster good communication between your staff and you
- identify poor performers and help them get on track, and
- lay the groundwork to fire poor performers lawfully and fairly if they don't improve.

The Value of Legal Knowledge

As you may have been told, conducting a shoddy performance appraisal can get your company—and you—into legal trouble. There's no point in sugarcoating it for you: Writing the wrong things on a performance appraisal or doing the appraisal unfairly or improperly can have devastating consequences if you are sued by an employee. Avoidable mistakes can cost your company a lot of money and cost you a lot of time and sleep—and even your job or reputation.

It behooves you, then, to gain a basic understanding of the legal principles that apply to performance appraisals so that you can avoid such mistakes. This book presents, in plain English, everything you need to know about the law as it applies to performance appraisals. Armed with this knowledge, you can conduct effective performance evaluations with confidence that you are on safe legal ground.

Who Wrote This Book

The people who created this book are not academics—they are employment lawyers, frontline managers, and human resource professionals. They know about performance appraisals from years of real-world experience. They bring a variety of perspectives to the information presented here.

Author Amy DelPo is an attorney who has represented employees in lawsuits against their employers and managers. In case after case, the performance evaluations played a pivotal role, either inoculating the company from liability because the manager did such an effective and fair job—or blowing the case wide open because the manager did something wrong. In addition to this experience, DelPo has spent countless hours speaking with employees, managers, and business owners and educating herself about the latest research on performance appraisal. She has written five books and numerous articles in the fields of employment law and human resources. In this, her latest book, DelPo applies her expert knowledge of performance appraisal systems to guide managers through what works, what doesn't, and what will either help or hurt if an employee decides to sue.

This book was reviewed by an advisory board made up of human resources professionals and managers who have designed and implemented performance evaluation systems in companies of all types and sizes. The advisory board members have learned through trial and error how to run appraisal systems that are as effective as they are legally sound. The board contributed valuable suggestions to the content of this book.

Who Should Read This Book

This book is for anyone who evaluates employee performance: managers, supervisors, executives, and human resources professionals. It tells you how to conduct performance appraisals that are effective and legally sound, within your company's existing systems.

This book is for people who work in private workplaces. Employment law operates slightly differently in government workplaces, and those differences are beyond the scope of this book.

If the employees of your company belong to one or more unions, much in this book will be useful to you. Be aware, however, that any collective bargaining agreement between a union and your company may change some of the legal rights and obligations described here and may require your performance evaluation system to differ from the one presented in this book. Do not rely on this book to interpret your collective bargaining agreement.

How to Use This Book

Think of this book as a companion to your company's performance appraisal system. Here you have the practical and legal guidance you need to work within your system and the law.

If this book ever conflicts with your system, you should follow your system and consult your human resources manager.

In each chapter, you will find several checklists to help you remember the important practical and legal principles involved in the task at hand. You can find tear-out versions of all the checklists and forms in Appendix B and on the CD-ROM at the back of the book. The CD also includes an interview with the author and a special bonus interview with Margie Mader-Clark, author of *The Job Description Handbook*, on using job descriptions as a performance management tool.

This book uses a model performance evaluation system, complete with forms and samples. If your company does not have a system in place, then you are free to use the forms we provide. If your company does have a system, however, you should use your company's forms.

Icons Used in This Book

 This icon alerts you to a practical tip or good idea.

 This icon is a caution to consider potential problems you may encounter.

 If you see this icon, there's a form in Appendix B (and on the CD-ROM at the back of the book) that will help you with the task at hand.

 This icon refers you to related information outside of this book—in other Nolo books or additional resources.

Chapter 1

An Overview of Performance Appraisal

Chapter Highlights

- Performance appraisal is a process, not a form. It structures your relationship with employees while providing legal protection for your company.

- A good appraisal system includes observation, documentation, and communication.

- A performance evaluation system can provide many benefits: It can improve employee performance and morale, identify poor performers and ways they can improve, and lay the groundwork for legally defensible discipline and termination.

- A manager's attitude helps determine whether a performance appraisal system will succeed. If the manager is enthusiastic about the chance to work with employees to improve their performance and their work experiences, the employees will share that enthusiasm.

- A good evaluation system includes support, motivation, communication, collaboration, fair treatment, documentation, formality, and accountability and is consistent with the company's core values and purpose.

- Managers should use evaluation systems to improve future performance, not punish employees for poor past performance.

- Employees must participate in every aspect of the evaluation process. Managers can increase employees' job satisfaction and engender their trust in the process by bringing them into the loop and giving them power and responsibility for directing and assessing their own performance.

- Managers must give feedback on an ongoing basis, not just at the year-end meeting. Managers must document employee performance as it occurs throughout the year.

- Although communicating negative information is difficult, not communicating it can be much worse.

I t's a common misconception that performance appraisal entails simply filling out an evaluation form—answering prefabricated questions and checking boxes. If this were the case, you wouldn't need an entire book to help you do it right, and your evaluation wouldn't be worth the paper you wrote it on.

When done correctly, performance appraisal is a process, not a document—it is a way of structuring your relationship with your employees. A good appraisal system includes observation, documentation, and communication. It envisions a workplace in which supervisors know what is happening in their departments (who is doing what and how well) and document employee performance as it occurs. Supervisors and their employees should have open lines of communication. Employees should know how they are doing so they can make adjustments when they veer off track. Supervisors should know what obstacles get in the way of their employees' performance so they can remove those obstacles as they arise.

Performance evaluations provide valuable continuity in a world where employees can change departments and managers during the course of a year. Often, a manager doesn't have the benefit of having observed an employee for the entire appraisal period. If every manager documents employee performance on an ongoing basis, the new manager can more easily pick up where the old manager left off.

Proper performance evaluations also provide important legal protection for your company and you. Sooner or later, despite your best efforts, you are bound to have difficulties with an employee. When this happens, an effective, legally sound performance evaluation system can serve as your first line of defense. Not only will it help you identify and deal with most employee problems before they rage out of control, it will also lay the groundwork for discipline and, if necessary, legally defensible termination when problems cannot be resolved.

Most lawsuits arise from the emotional state of the employee. Employees who feel treated unfairly or who are surprised by an unfavorable management decision are more likely to complain and to sue. Performance evaluations make the workplace more fair and predictable, thereby reducing the chances of disgruntled—and, therefore, litigious—employees.

This chapter provides an overview of performance evaluation systems by exploring their benefits, considering the qualities shared by effective systems, and introducing you to the steps in the model system this book presents.

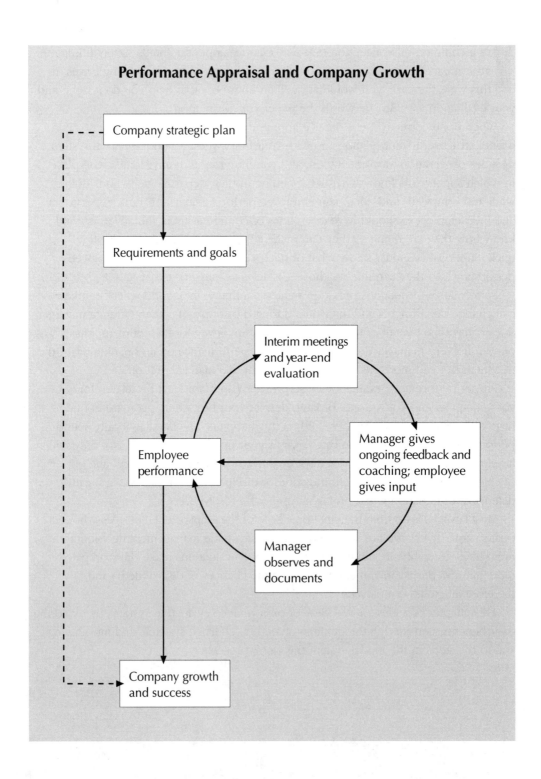

Performance Appraisal and Company Growth

The Benefits of a Performance Evaluation System

Most successful supervisors share common goals and challenges, including how to tap into the potential of each employee. You understand that your company benefits when employees feel like part of a team—loyal to their coworkers, their company, and you (their manager). As you know, it's sound policy to reward good employees, encourage productive employees to strive for more, and help wayward employees get back on track. And, on occasion, you will need to let go of problem employees who, despite all efforts, cannot or will not do their jobs satisfactorily.

An effective performance appraisal system will help you achieve all of these ends—and more—by providing a solid foundation for all aspects of the employer/employee relationship. Such a system can help you:

- determine how the job of each employee can further the overall goals of the organization
- examine each employee as an individual to evaluate the employee's strengths and weaknesses
- identify and reward good employees, in order to foster loyalty and motivate employees to continue to achieve
- keep employee morale high through continuous feedback
- stay on top of the needs of your workforce to ensure employee retention and increase productivity and innovation
- reduce the risk of complaints and litigation by ensuring that employees feel treated fairly and are not surprised by management decisions, and
- identify and deal with problem employees to either turn those employees into valuable, productive workers or lay the groundwork for discipline and, if necessary, termination.

All of this translates into better employee performance, which leads to better departmental performance, which leads to a more successful company. Indeed, an entire body of current research connects performance evaluation systems like the one described in this book to improved employee—and company—performance.

This book often revisits the benefits you can gain from an effective performance evaluation system. The rules this book presents are designed to ensure that you reap all of these benefits from your own system.

What's Not to Like?

Having to complete performance evaluations is the thing many managers like the least about their jobs. Given the known benefits of effective performance appraisal, what makes it so unpopular?

A big reason is that it takes time, especially if it is done well. Managers view performance evaluations as time wasted pushing paper instead of doing "real" work. But if part or all of your job is to manage employees, performance appraisal is not only real work—it is an essential part of your job.

Often, the performance evaluation process is the only time set aside for formal communication with your employees about their work. If you follow the guidance in this book, the time you spend on the performance appraisal process will pay for itself many times over with improvements to the efficiency, productivity, performance, and morale of your employees.

Another reason managers dislike performance appraisal is the discomfort they feel when confronting employees about poor performance. While communicating negative information is difficult, not communicating it can be much worse. An uncomfortable, but clear, conversation with a poor performer can prevent you from making big mistakes, such as:

- allowing employees to work under the mistaken belief that they are doing well, thereby never giving them the information they need to improve
- tolerating poor performers and the burdens they place on your other employees and your company
- surprising poor performers with negative decisions, and
- facing difficulty in terminating bad employees because you have not laid the proper groundwork.

Lack of training or having to work within a flawed system are other reasons managers dislike performance evaluations. Some managers have spent years conducting performance evaluations that seem ineffective, illogical, or meaningless. They haven't seen the benefits that a complete, effective, and consistent appraisal system can bring to their company. Fortunately, applying the rules presented in this book can help.

Finally, fear of the unspecified legal consequences of performance evaluations makes managers uncomfortable. Many managers have been warned that they can get their company and themselves into legal trouble if they don't do things correctly, but nobody explains what that means. This book clearly explains the legal consequences of performance evaluations.

The Elements of an Effective System

This book is designed to complement the performance appraisal system already in place at your company. These systems have an infinite number of variations, so the discussion here won't always match what you find in your company's system. For example, the terms used here may not match the terms your company uses, or your company may require coordination with your human resources department, something this book does not discuss. Your company may have a single place for storing performance records, whereas the system described here assumes that managers keep their own files.

Although you should pay attention to these differences—and follow your company's rules—know that most of these variations are cosmetic. All effective performance appraisal systems share the same basic qualities, and those are the themes that you should take away from this book and apply to the system in place at your company.

This section discusses some specific qualities that all effective performance evaluation systems share, paying particular attention to those that you as a manager can control.

A Fair and Communicative Environment

The most effective performance appraisal systems place concern for the employee at their core. The reality is that you cannot control your employees' behavior—only they control how they perform their jobs. Research has shown, however, that the majority of employees want to perform well; the key is to provide them with the right environment in which to do so. Such an environment includes support, communication, collaboration, and fair treatment—the very qualities created by effective performance appraisal systems. In addition, a fair and communicative environment builds employee morale.

Respect for the Employee

You can follow every step in this book, but if you don't demonstrate a fundamental respect for your employees, you will fail. This respect is the foundation for any effective performance evaluation system. Employees who feel respected are more likely to buy into the appraisal system—to participate fully and sincerely in setting goals and to strive hard to perform to the standards you set. On the other hand, employees who don't feel respected will show that same lack of respect for you and your efforts to improve their performance.

Money, Money, Money

Some companies connect performance appraisal to salary review; others don't. Tying the two together is a subject of some controversy. Obviously, you must follow your company's procedures. But if you have some say in the matter, you might consider the following reasons some companies choose to keep performance appraisal and salary review separate.

Studies show that appraisals linked to administrative goals (such as salary increases) are less accurate than those linked to developmental goals (such as improving employee and team performance). This makes sense: The performance evaluation process is supposed to be about employee development. If the end result of the evaluation is a change in salary, employees may become less focused on development and more focused on end results. Employees may listen only to the money part of an evaluation and ignore the development part.

Another great benefit of performance appraisal is the feedback managers get from employees. If employees know that their raises hang in the balance, they may not be as forthcoming.

Also, instead of pushing themselves to strive for goals that are just out of reach, employees may rein in their goals so that they can be sure of meeting them—and of snagging a raise when they are reviewed.

Finally, some managers may have a gut feeling about who should get a raise—a feeling often based on soft factors such as whom they like and whom they relate to best. Linking a raise to a performance review can be risky because a manager may—consciously or not—write the appraisal to support the raise decision, rather than base the decision on the appraisal. In such cases, neither the salary decisions nor the reviews make much sense. And if a lawsuit arises, the appraisal may not adequately explain why a certain employee got a raise but another did not.

Focus on the Future

If, at its heart, a performance appraisal process is designed to improve employee performance, then a manager should emphasize what the employee can do going forward, not how the employee did in the past. The past can inform your ideas about the future, but it shouldn't be the sole focus of the appraisal process.

This means that you should spend the bulk of the appraisal meeting on identifying goals for the next year and talking about how the employee can achieve them. It also means that your feedback throughout the year should not punish or shame employees for bad performance, but help employees see when their performance is slipping and strategize with them on how to improve. This doesn't mean that looking at past performance has no place in the process; indeed, at each evaluation you should discuss whether and how the employee met the goals set at the previous evaluation. But you should look to the past with the goal of learning from it, so that the look backward is developmental and helpful to the employee, rather than punitive.

Employee Participation

Another element common to successful performance evaluation systems is employee participation. Employees must play a key role, participating in everything from writing job descriptions, to identifying their own goals and standards, to assessing how well they have performed.

You can increase employees' job satisfaction and engender their trust in the appraisal system by bringing them into the loop and giving them power and responsibility for directing and assessing their own performance. This satisfaction and trust leads employees to accept the company's appraisal process and make a commitment to their own development.

In addition, you need the information that your employees can bring to the table. Your employees are often in the best position to answer the questions posed during the appraisal process; at the very least, they can provide some crucial insights. These questions include:

- How can they help the company achieve its goals?
- How much can be expected from someone in a given job?
- Are there any organizational impediments to their performance?
- Is there anything you can provide to help them perform better?
- How well have they achieved their own goals?

Research has shown that when employees are involved in goal setting, the goals they set are higher and more demanding than goals that managers set alone. Employees will push the envelope, often demanding more of themselves than you might demand of them.

Employee participation promotes teamwork. It gives the two of you the sense of working together rather than being on opposite sides of the fence. It also reduces the chances that you will miss out on important information or insights you could share with each other.

Ongoing Feedback

Giving employees feedback—both positive and negative—as circumstances warrant is another important feature of an effective performance evaluation system. If you tell employees what you think of their performance only once a year, you've wasted a lot of opportunities throughout the year to encourage good performance and to help employees who are struggling get back on track.

Feedback also helps employees adjust as circumstances change throughout the year. The importance of certain goals may shift; obstacles may appear; employees may lose motivation or focus. Your feedback will tell employees what is still important, what is no longer important, and what they can do to achieve their goals in the face of these changes.

Studies have shown that without feedback, a performance appraisal system alone will not improve employee performance. Positive feedback, often particularly neglected, is important: Providing positive feedback whenever appropriate gives employees a sense of accomplishment and appreciation, while highlighting standards for how they should continue to perform.

Document, Document, Document

Ongoing and accurate documentation is the crux of a good performance appraisal system. Documentation spanning the entire appraisal period ensures that your review will be fair and accurate and gives you rock-solid support in case of a lawsuit. Without good documentation of an employee's performance throughout the year, all you'll have are memories and gut feelings, neither of which are reliable or legally safe.

In addition, good documentation provides continuity should the employee change departments or managers. If the old manager properly documented the employee's performance, the new manager can take over more easily than if no record existed.

This book provides you with a method for documenting employee performance throughout the year that does not require too much time or effort. In fact, following the suggested methods in this book will actually save you time and make the appraisal process easier in the long run. With proper documentation, you can avoid once and for all the horrible feeling of having to write a year-end appraisal for an employee whose performance you can barely recall.

Your Role

Performance appraisal is not a human resources issue; it's a management issue. For that reason, you—as the manager—are the key to its success. You must buy into the process and commit to it. Your role in the process includes, of course, following any steps required by your company's system. Regardless of the system your company uses, to do this well you must set standards and goals, observe and document performance, give feedback, and conduct appraisal meetings.

Your role goes beyond these duties, however. As a manager responsible for implementing the performance evaluation system, you are like a bridge between the company and the employee. You must be friend to both, always mindful of the company's overall needs and strategic plan while at the same time acting as something of an advocate for your employees. Although this is tricky and somewhat controversial, it's important, because both your company and your team need you. You should work to create an environment in which your employees— and the company as a whole—can perform at their best.

As such, your attitude is key to the success of the process. If you think that performance appraisal is an annoying waste of time, your employees will, too. If, on the other hand, you are enthusiastic and optimistic about the chance to work with your employees to improve their performance and their experiences at work, many of your employees will share in your enthusiasm. If you think the appraisal system is worthwhile, so will they. If you commit yourself to it, you increase the likelihood that they will, too. Your style and vision in laying the proper foundation for performance management will determine in large part whether the system succeeds or fails.

To motivate your employees to perform well, you must do more than just provide an encouraging word here or there (though encouraging words certainly help). For employees to commit to their jobs and have the desire to perform well, some or all of the following must occur:

- They must feel that their jobs give them the opportunity to accomplish something that is important or worthwhile.
- They must have the resources they need to do their jobs and meet their standards and goals.
- They must receive feedback so that they always know what is expected of them and whether they are meeting those expectations.
- They must receive recognition for what they do. Although this recognition should include raises and bonuses, it's just as important to recognize employees in nonmonetary ways—for example, through a positive write-up in the company newsletter, a memo commending the employee on a job well done that you copy to company higher-ups, or an announcement of praise at a company meeting.
- They must be given the opportunity to grow and develop. They should not be asked to do things they simply cannot do (because, for example, they don't have the skills or the resources), but they should be challenged by their jobs and asked to do more and different things. They must feel a comfortable stretch when accomplishing some of their tasks.
- They must gain autonomy and responsibility as they demonstrate their abilities.
- They must feel free to express their opinions and ideas about their jobs, any obstacles to performance, and how the company can run better.
- Management must listen to them.
- They must feel like an important part of the company's success.

Obviously, you aren't in control of all of these factors, but you are in control of a number of them. For example, you can give recognition and you can, and should, listen. You can also work hard to get the resources your employees need. Although you can't change job descriptions fundamentally, you can increase a person's responsibility as that person demonstrates an ability and desire to take on new responsibilities. For example, are there things on your own to-do list that you could assign to an employee you supervise instead of doing yourself?

Model Appraisal System

This book guides you through a model performance appraisal system, devoting a chapter to each step you should take along the way. The system at your workplace may not exactly match the one presented in this book. Virtually all appraisal systems, however, will contain some or all of the steps that this book discusses:

- Work with employees to set job-related goals and standards for their performance. Chapter 3 shows you how.
- Regularly observe and document employee performance in relation to these goals and standards. Chapter 4 gives you the tools you need.
- Meet with employees periodically to discuss their performance and to redefine their goals, if necessary. Chapters 4 and 5 explain how.
- Conduct a formal performance appraisal at the end of each year. Chapter 6 covers this step.

Before moving into a discussion of each step you should take, Chapter 2 pauses to explain the legal consequences of performance evaluations and common legal traps that you—and your company—can avoid.

Responsibilities in a Performance Appraisal System	
The company	• Creates the strategic plan • Provides support and resources
The manager	• Identifies job requirements • Observes and documents employee performance • Provides ongoing feedback to the employee • Provides support and resources
The manager and the employee together	• Identify job goals • Create action plans for how to meet requirements and goals • Engage in ongoing dialogue about employee performance
The employee	• Listens to and acts on feedback from the manager • Performs by meeting requirements and goals • Provides feedback to the manager about the work environment

Test Your Knowledge

Questions

1. The written, year-end evaluation is the most important aspect of a performance appraisal system.   ☐ True ☐ False

2. You are in control of your employees' performance.   ☐ True ☐ False

3. Your primary focus in doing a performance evaluation is to review each task an employee did in the past year to assess how well he or she performed.   ☐ True ☐ False

4. Employee involvement in a performance evaluation is limited to listening to what you have to say and following your instructions.   ☐ True ☐ False

5. Employees often know more than you do about their jobs and how well they have performed them.   ☐ True ☐ False

6. If you allow employees to participate in setting their own performance goals, they will set easier goals for themselves than you would set for them.   ☐ True ☐ False

7. You should give employees feedback throughout the year, not just at formal, year-end reviews.   ☐ True ☐ False

8. If you have a good memory, documentation is a waste of time.   ☐ True ☐ False

9. Documentation can help you in case of a lawsuit.   ☐ True ☐ False

10. If your company's system isn't the same as the one described in this book, the book will be useless to you.   ☐ True ☐ False

Answers

1. **False.** Performance appraisal is a process, not a piece of paper. No part of the process is the most important; all aspects of the system work together.

2. **False.** You can guide employees and control many of the circumstances they encounter, but ultimately, only employees control how they perform.

3. **False.** You should look toward the future, not dwell on the past. You and the employee can learn from what happened over the past year, but focusing on it too much destroys the evaluation's use as a developmental tool.

4. **False.** Employees should, of course, listen and follow instructions, but their role in performance appraisal is much broader. Each employee should play an integral role in his or her own performance evaluation process, from setting goals to assessing his or her own performance.

5. **True.** Employees are often on the front line of your business. You can learn a lot from them about what happens in your workplace, what obstacles they face, and how they are performing.

6. **False.** In a workplace that uses an effective performance evaluation system, employees tend to set higher goals for themselves than their managers would set for them.

7. **True.** Ongoing feedback, both positive and negative, is an important aspect of a successful performance evaluation system.

8. **False.** No matter how good your memory, documenting employee performance as it occurs will give you a much more detailed, accurate, and reliable picture of an employee's performance over the course of an entire year. Also, documentation is necessary to create a record that supports your actions in case of a lawsuit.

9. **True.** If someone sues your company, what you say won't be worth much if you don't have evidence to back it up; documentation can provide that evidence. A clear, written record that supports your statements and explains your actions can go a long way toward protecting your company—and you—if an employee sues.

10. **False.** All effective appraisal systems share some or all of the steps, and most of the principles, discussed in this book. Understanding the model performance appraisal system presented here will make you a better manager and a better participant in your company's performance evaluation process.

■

Chapter 2

Legal Traps

Chapter Highlights

- The strategies you use to make your performance appraisal system fair and effective (honest communication, regular feedback, accuracy and precision, consistent documentation, objectivity, and respect for employees) will also make your system legally sound.

- Most employees who work for your company do so on what is called an "at-will" basis. This means that you can fire them at any time for any reason that isn't illegal, and they can quit at any time for any reason.

- You can jeopardize this at-will status by making promises during the performance evaluation process. You should avoid telling employees anything that sounds like a guarantee of future employment—for example, that they "have a future at the company" or "have a job as long as they keep up the good work."

- The right to terminate employees without having to prove that you had "just cause" to do so is an important one, and it can make the difference between winning and losing a wrongful termination lawsuit.

- If you fire an employee, the employee's performance evaluations must support—or, at the very least, not contradict—your reasons for the termination. In evaluations, you must tell the truth, be thorough, and anticipate trouble. Not only is this a way to make your evaluations more fair and effective, but it gives you legal protection as well.

- Writing things that could be viewed as discriminatory or harassing in a performance evaluation can lead to a lawsuit. Avoid racial slurs, jokes, and stereotypes. Be specific about your criticisms. Differences based on characteristics protected by law—such as race, gender, national origin, religion, age, or disability—should not enter into your thinking.

- If an employee mentions a physical or mental problem to you, consult with your human resources department or legal counsel.

- Don't retaliate against employees for complaining about discrimination, harassment, or illegal conduct; for filing a workers' compensation claim; for serving as a witness for a coworker's complaint or claim; or for otherwise asserting their rights under employment laws. It's against the law.

- Document, document, document. In addition to the practical reasons to keep records (discussed in Chapter 4), proper documentation can help you prove your side of the case if you get sued.

In any wrongful termination or employment discrimination lawsuit, one of the first things the employee's attorney will ask for are the employee's performance evaluations. The attorney is digging for the piece of evidence that will prove the employee's case or disprove the employer's case—and in many situations, that's exactly what the attorney will find. It's amazing how many evaluations contain the proverbial smoking gun that makes an employee's case. Perhaps the evaluation uses racial slurs or stereotypes, or maybe it directly contradicts the reasons the company now asserts for terminating the employee. Whatever the legal gaffe, a manager with a basic understanding of the law would not have fallen into the same trap.

The good news is that you don't have to do a lot of extra work just to safeguard against the relatively rare event of a lawsuit. Many of the rules you must follow to keep your appraisals within the bounds of the law are the same rules this book describes for effective performance appraisal. Thus, you can kill two birds with one stone, so to speak, by following the practices described in this book. Specifically:

- You must communicate honestly with your employees.
- You must provide your employees with regular feedback.
- Your evaluations must be accurate and precise.
- You must document everything you say and conclude.
- All of your statements must be related to the job the employee performs.
- You must always treat employees with consideration and respect.

As you continue to read this book, you will learn more about these rules and how they help make performance evaluations effective, fair, and, as a bonus, lawful.

For an added measure of security, this chapter alerts you to the most common legal traps you face when writing performance evaluations—and tells you how to avoid them. Armed with this knowledge and with the guidelines provided throughout the remainder of this book, your company and you will be on safe legal ground when conducting performance appraisals.

The truth is, however, that lawsuits are relatively rare. Don't get too wrapped up in worrying about preventing them. As long as you follow good management practices to create a good and positive work environment for your employees, and you keep in mind the tips in this chapter, you'll be just fine.

Don't undermine your review in nonreview situations. This chapter addresses only the performance evaluation process: the written evaluation and the interim and year-end evaluation meetings. But any time you discuss performance with an employee, even in less formal situations, you should be aware of these legal traps. For example, company-sponsored parties are events where you may be tempted to become collegial with team members who are having a performance problem. You might want to soften the blow of a recently given negative performance review—either for the employee's sake or because you don't want the employee to be angry with you. Either way, try not to backpedal from your review. Otherwise, you undermine it—both practically and legally.

Don't Destroy the At-Will Relationship

Most of the employees who work for you do so on an "at-will" basis. This means that neither they, nor the company, are bound to any sort of employment contract, and, when you terminate them, you do not have to worry about having any specific justification to do so. At-will employees can quit at any time for any reason, and you can fire them at any time for any reason that isn't illegal. Reasons for terminating employees that are not legal include, for example, firing employees because of their race or age or because they refused to work in hazardous conditions or off the clock.

Instead of having an at-will relationship with its employees, a company can create a situation in which it can only fire the employee for "just cause." This means that the employer must have a legitimate business-related reason for firing the employee, such as poor performance, low productivity, violent behavior, or a legitimate layoff or downsizing.

The default employment status of most workers is at-will. To change it, the employer must create a contract, either by something it writes or something it says (through its executives and managers) that implies that the employee's job is secure.

If you need more information. For a comprehensive discussion of employment law as it relates to managing employees, including legal and illegal reasons for termination, at-will employment, and employment contracts, see *Dealing With Problem Employees*, by Amy DelPo and Lisa Guerin (Nolo).

At-will employees are easier to fire because you don't have to prove that you had just cause for the firing. You can fire at-will employees for any reason that isn't illegal—for example, you don't think they contribute much or they are mean to their coworkers—or for no reason at all. The only thing you need to consider and prepare for before firing an at-will employee is how to counter any claim that the firing was illegal.

This right to terminate employees without having to prove just cause is an important one, and it can make the difference between winning and losing a wrongful termination lawsuit. Prudent employers—and their managers—guard the at-will status of their employees carefully.

Unfortunately for employers, an employment contract destroying the at-will relationship doesn't have to be signed by the employer, or even written on a piece of paper. Managers can create such an employment contract unintentionally through the things they say to employees—things that imply a promise of continued employment. If you make statements to an employee, either verbally or by writing them in a performance evaluation, that contradict the no-strings-attached terms of an at-will relationship, you may create an employment contract that destroys the at-will relationship, even though you don't intend to. You could create such an implied contract if, for example, you tell an employee something like, "For as long as I run this department, there will be a job for you here."

Performance appraisal is one situation in which managers can destroy the at-will relationship without meaning to. In a well-meaning but misguided attempt to compliment the employee or to convey how important the employee is to the company, the manager might make promises or use language that implies a commitment beyond the at-will relationship that currently exists.

Consider the following statements made by managers during performance evaluations. The language in italics is particularly problematic and could destroy the at-will relationship:

- "Paul's work is consistently excellent. *He has a bright future at this company.*"
- "Jane recorded higher-than-expected sales for the fourth consecutive quarter. If she continues to perform at these levels, *she could be senior vice president for sales within the next two years.*"
- "For as long as Mya continues to perform at these levels, *she will have a job in this company.*"
- "As usual, Sara didn't disappoint during this review period. *If she continues on this performance trajectory, there's no telling how far she will go in this company.*"
- "Omar is a pleasure to work with. *I hope that he remains at this company for a long time.*"
- "All of Juan's coworkers love working with him. *We hope he makes this company his professional home for the rest of his career.*"
- "Lily seems unsure about her future here. *I reassured her that her job was secure.*"

Beyond the legal implications of undermining the at-will relationship, on a personal level it's unfair and unkind to give employees a false sense of security. Although it's appropriate and even mandatory for you to praise an employee for a job well done, don't add a promise to the praise; that way, everyone understands the rules of the relationship and a fired employee will be less likely to bring a wrongful termination lawsuit. Even if you mean what you say, you don't have a crystal ball. You can't know that the relationship won't go sour, that the employee won't develop troubling work habits, or that the company won't someday need to trim its workforce. If you stick to talking about the employee's performance—that is, how the employee has performed in the past and what goals and requirements you expect the employee to meet in the future—your evaluations will not destroy the at-will relationship.

Don't Undermine Potential Terminations

If you fire an employee, the employee's performance evaluations must support—or at the very least not contradict—the reasons you give for the firing. And, because you can't go back and create evaluations after someone is fired, you must write evaluations with this rule in mind, even if you have no current plans to terminate the employee.

Consider the following examples—all taken from real-life cases—in which performance evaluations played a significant role.

> **EXAMPLE 1:** A hospital fires an African-American doctor. She does not have an employment contract, so the hospital does not need just cause to fire her. Nonetheless, the doctor files a wrongful termination lawsuit, claiming that she was fired because of her race. When she files her lawsuit, she has no real evidence of racial discrimination; her case is based on her belief that she was always treated more harshly than her coworkers, most of whom were white men. The hospital responds by asserting that she was fired because of her poor diagnostic skills and her inability to get along with her coworkers. Her attorney requests her performance evaluations.
>
> Unfortunately for the hospital, the doctor's evaluations all give her good marks for diagnostic skills—not the highest ratings, but certainly acceptable ones—and none of them mentions personality difficulties. In fact, one specifically praises the doctor for how well she works with the nurses and staff. Even though the doctor still has no proof of racial discrimination, she

now has evidence that makes hospital management look like it's lying about why it fired her. And the argument her attorney will make to a jury is that the only reason to lie is to cover up illegal motives for the termination, such as racial discrimination. The hospital knows a losing case when it sees one and settles the case before trial.

EXAMPLE 2: A company fires a computer programmer, claiming that he has a difficult and disruptive personality. The programmer believes he was fired because he complained to superiors about the company's illegal practice of using copyrighted software without a license. Although the programmer was an at-will employee, he files a wrongful termination case because he believes he was fired for an illegal reason (his complaint about the company's illegal conduct). The programmer's performance evaluations do not praise his personality, but none of them mention any difficulties.

The case goes to trial, and the programmer's attorney asks the jury to consider the obvious question: If the company had a problem with the programmer's personality, why didn't this issue show up on any of his evaluations? The answer, the attorney suggests, is that the company is lying to cover up its illegal motives for the termination. The jury is convinced, and the programmer wins the case.

EXAMPLE 3: A doctors' office fires a nurse, claiming that she is often late, doesn't carry her share of the workload, and is rude to patients. The nurse, who has an employment contract that says she cannot be fired without just cause, sues. Although all of the reasons asserted by the office constitute just cause, the office must now prove them in the lawsuit. The nurse's performance evaluations are silent on all of the relevant issues and are, in fact, generally positive about her medical skills. The doctors' office does, however, have other evidence of the nurse's tardiness—her timesheets—and has some written complaints from patients to support its claim that she was rude. Regardless, the fact that her performance evaluations were silent on these issues presents a hurdle the doctors' office must overcome.

In the end, the office decides to settle the case, feeling insecure about whether it can convince a jury of its position in light of what it did not include in the nurse's performance evaluations.

In each of these cases, and hundreds more like them each year, the employee's performance evaluations sunk the company for one of two reasons: They either (1) directly contradicted the company's asserted reasons for firing the employee, or (2) were silent on the subject of the company's asserted reasons for firing the employee.

Each of these cases would likely have swung the other way if only the manager conducting the employee's evaluations had done a better job. Who knows why the evaluations in these cases didn't support the company's stated reasons for firing the employee? Perhaps the manager was trying to be kind and spare the employee's feelings, or perhaps the manager didn't have a good grasp of the employee's performance problems or was never trained properly on the importance of effective performance appraisal.

Whatever the reason, the lessons are clear:

- **Tell the truth.** A performance evaluation is not the place to spare an employee's feelings or ignore poor conduct just because you want to avoid confrontation. There's no need to use harsh language or be cruel, but you must be clear, precise, and frank about the employee's performance. This is an important part of your job as a manager or supervisor. If you gloss over the negative and emphasize the positive because you want to be nice, you will do more damage in the long run and compromise your ability to fire the employee should the need arise.

- **Be thorough.** The performance appraisal process is not the time to take shortcuts. Collect your thoughts and documentation before you sit down to write the evaluation. (Chapter 4 tells you how to document, and Chapter 6 guides you through the process of writing an evaluation.) After you are done writing, read through the evaluation to make sure that you have covered all aspects of the employee's performance and included anything you think should be documented.

- **Anticipate trouble.** If an employee is becoming a problem and you think a termination is on the horizon, lay the groundwork for firing the employee in the evaluation. Obviously, you should never lie or embellish the truth in doing this. But you should make sure that the things that make you think a termination is likely are reflected in the evaluation and supported by documentation.

Of course, if there is nothing wrong with the employee's performance, then it's fine to have a review that is entirely positive. Just make sure that the positive review is earned and not a product of your glossing over poor performance.

Don't Harass or Discriminate

A variety of federal and state laws prohibits discrimination and harassment in employment. Discrimination occurs when you treat someone differently on the basis of some characteristic, such as race, gender, disability, and so on. It may be perfectly legal to treat people differently based on some characteristics, but not based on others. If a characteristic is specifically listed in an antidiscrimination law, then it is illegal to discriminate against someone on the basis of that characteristic. These are called "protected characteristics."

Federal law prohibits discrimination on the basis of race, gender (including pregnancy), national origin (including affiliation with a Native American tribe), religion, disability, and age (if the person is at least 40 years old). (To learn more about federal antidiscrimination laws, see Appendix C.)

State and local laws often prohibit additional types of discrimination, including discrimination on the basis of marital status, sexual orientation, and weight. (To find out what forms of discrimination are illegal in your state, see "State Laws Prohibiting Discrimination in Private Employment" in Appendix C.)

Harassment is a type of discrimination. The same laws that prohibit discrimination on the basis of protected characteristics also prohibit harassment on the basis of those characteristics. Harassment occurs when an employee or group of employees must endure a work environment that is hostile, offensive, or intimidating to them because they have a protected characteristic. Sexual harassment is probably the best-known type of harassment, but workers can be harassed on the basis of whatever makes them different, including race, religion, or sexual orientation.

Things that could constitute harassment include, for example, epithets or slurs, mockery, demeaning jokes and cartoons, extreme unwarranted criticism, implied or explicit threats of violence, or requiring an employee to do something in return for favorable (or not unfavorable) treatment. While harassment often involves racial epithets or sexual innuendos, it does not have to do so to be illegal. Treating employees in a generally hostile or demeaning way simply because of their protected characteristic is also harassment—for example, a supervisor constantly criticizing, demeaning, or requiring more from his only African-American employee while being supportive and helpful to white employees.

It should go without saying (but unfortunately it does not): Do not use any language that could be considered harassing or discriminatory in performance evaluations. Obviously, this means not to use any racial slurs or sexual language;

do not, in fact, mention any protected characteristic, such as the employee's age, gender, race, national origin, disability, sexual orientation, and so on unless you have a good business-related reason for doing so.

But even beyond this, you must avoid subtle language or conclusions that might appear to be based on stereotypes about people who share a protected characteristic. Even if you do not intend to discriminate or harass, you may be accused of it if you don't choose your words with care.

Some words that seem innocuous can actually be code words that could indicate bias. For example, sometimes when people say an employee is "different" or "doesn't fit in," they mean that the employee is different because of a protected characteristic. Similarly, when managers say that an employee "makes coworkers uncomfortable," sometimes what they really mean is that the coworkers don't like working with someone of a different race, gender, religion, or background. This is a problem, because differences based on protected characteristics should not enter into your thinking. Always be specific enough in your feedback that you spell out a job-related problem: The fact that someone is different or does things differently doesn't identify a problem with the person's work.

The chart below offers some examples of language that could be construed as discriminatory and how to rewrite it to focus on job-related, rather than personal, characteristics.

The comments listed in the chart may not be terribly shocking, but each could create problems if the employee brings a discrimination case against your company. When reviewing employee performance, think freely; before you write your ideas down or discuss them with the employee, however, think carefully. If your first thought is, for example, "David doesn't fit in here," identify why you think that before you write it down. Is it because David is different from his coworkers based on a protected characteristic (for example, he is an African-American person among mostly white people), or because of a job-related characteristic (for example, he is not good at public speaking, something that is a big part of his job)? If it is the former, you cannot criticize him for "not fitting in" solely because he is of a different race; not only is it unfair and entirely unrelated to his job performance, but it is illegal. If it is the latter, then be specific in your feedback. Focus on the job-related behavior or traits, not the characteristic.

To steer clear of legal trouble, observe the following guidelines:

- Do not focus on the fact that someone is different because of a protected characteristic.

Choose Your Words Carefully: Problematic Phrases and How to Fix Them	
Don't Say	**Do Say**
John is really stuck in his ways. I guess you can't teach an old dog new tricks. **Issue: Age discrimination**	John's performance has failed to improve despite attending a training session and despite my repeated attempts to coach him on our new procedures.
Mary is out of step with today's marketing styles and doesn't seem to understand young people. **Issue: Age discrimination**	Mary's marketing ideas do not seem to be resonating with our target audience. Focus groups of our target markets did not respond well to Mary's ideas.
Lila doesn't put enough effort into how she looks. If she dressed up and wore makeup, customers in the store would respond to her better. **Issue: Gender discrimination**	Lila needs to project a more polished, professional image when dealing with customers.
Marquis doesn't have the same energy and vitality that he used to have. He is becoming a lot less productive. **Issue: Age discrimination**	Marquis's productivity has dropped off in recent years, as indicated by the attached reports.
Laurence seems stuck in the past. None of his advertising ideas have appealed to our clients, who are looking for a youthful perspective. They are taking their business to other firms considered to be more cutting edge. **Issue: Age discrimination**	Laurence needs to improve his ability to understand and meet our clients' needs. A number of clients have rejected Laurence's advertising campaigns repeatedly in the past year and have moved their business to other firms.
Abigail does a good job on her own, but she doesn't work well with the rest of the team. She sticks to herself and isn't willing to be one of the guys. **Issue: Gender discrimination**	Abigail needs to improve her rapport with coworkers and her ability to work with her team.

Choose Your Words Carefully: Problematic Phrases and How to Fix Them (cont'd)	
Don't Say	**Do Say**
Betina has trouble being assertive because she is the only woman on her project. She should not let that fact prevent her from speaking up at meetings, because she has a lot of good ideas. **Issue: Gender discrimination**	Betina should speak up more at meetings, because she has a lot of good ideas.
Sabrina is too emotional. The rest of the guys have trouble approaching her because she seems so touchy. **Issue: Gender discrimination**	Sabrina needs to improve her communication with coworkers.
Joan is too pushy. She can be domineering in meetings and her coworkers feel bowled over by her. **Issue: Gender discrimination**	Joan needs to pay attention to the others on her team to make sure they have a chance to contribute.
Patrick doesn't fit our image of what a leader should be. **Issue: Race or national origin discrimination**	Patrick has not demonstrated the following qualities that we think are necessary to lead...
Marcus makes his coworkers uncomfortable—he doesn't seem to fit in here. **Issue: Race or national origin discrimination**	Marcus has done the following things that have resulted in the following coworker complaints...
Amy's ethnic background makes her seem rude. **Issue: Race or national origin discrimination**	We have received the following customer complaints about Amy...
Because of Mildred's religious beliefs, she won't socialize with her clients at bars. This has affected her sales numbers. **Issue: Religious discrimination**	Mildred's sales numbers are too low. She needs to make a better effort to cultivate her client relationships.

- Never ever use slurs or demeaning language in performance evaluations—even if you think you are being funny.
- Do not mention protected characteristics.
- Do not make assumptions about employees that are based on stereotypes about protected characteristics.
- Avoid vague language that stresses that an employee is different—that he or she "doesn't fit in" or "isn't one of us."
- State facts, not conclusions. For example, it's fine to say that someone is not productive or not performing well, but do not give an explanation that touches on a protected characteristic—for example, because of the employee's age or disability.
- Be specific. If you include documented details, people will have more difficulty attributing your statements to discrimination or harassment.
- Stick to statements that are related to the job. This will ensure that you don't veer into illegal territory. For example, if a female employee is always late, it's fine to state that, but don't add your irrelevant belief that she is late because she has children.
- If coworkers or customers don't like an employee because of a protected characteristic, the problem lies with the coworkers or customers, not the employee. You should not criticize the employee for an inability to get along with those coworkers or customers.
- Focus on behavior, not the person. Discriminatory bias is about who people are, not what they do. If you focus on actions, you'll steer clear of hidden biases.

Even the most well-intentioned managers can fall prey to hidden biases, ones even they may not be aware exist. When conducting performance appraisals, be careful not to judge employees like you (or employees you like) more favorably, to judge employees different from you (or employees you dislike) less favorably, or to engage in stereotyping. Although often difficult, being honest with yourself about biases can save your company and you money and headaches.

Special Rules Regarding Disabilities

State and federal laws protect the right of people with disabilities to work. These laws impose two separate duties on employers.

First, an employer cannot base employment decisions on the fact that someone has a disability. This is a straightforward prohibition against disability discrimination, similar to laws that forbid other forms of illegal discrimination, such as discrimination based on race or sex.

Second, if an employee has a disability and can do the job with an accommodation from you, then you have an obligation to provide that accommodation, as long as it is reasonable—that is, it doesn't cost too much or create too much of an inconvenience for the company. Accommodating a worker means providing assistance or making changes in the job or workplace that will enable the worker to do the job. For example, an employer might lower the height of a desktop to accommodate a worker in a wheelchair, provide TDD telephone equipment for a worker whose hearing is impaired, or provide a quiet, distraction-free workspace for a worker with attention deficit disorder.

Disability laws are quite complicated, and knowing whether someone has a disability or what type of accommodation to provide can require legal and technical analyses that you, as a manager, are not equipped to make. For your purposes, be aware that if you notice an employee's performance is suffering because of a physical or mental problem, or if an employee mentions a physical or mental problem to you, a little alarm should go off in your brain and you should consult with your human resources department or legal counsel about what to do.

If you know or suspect that an employee may have a physical or mental disability, it is important that you go through the process of accommodating the employee before you engage in the performance appraisal process described in this book. When you write a performance evaluation on an employee with a disability, you should have already consulted with your human resources department or legal counsel so that you understand your rights and responsibilities as a supervisor managing that employee.

Don't Retaliate

When an employee complains about discrimination, harassment, or another violation of a workplace law (for example, health and safety standards), or if an employee backs up another employee's complaint, you must treat the employee with care. If you take any action that the employee might view as punishment or retribution for the complaint—including giving the employee a negative performance evaluation because of the complaint—you might find yourself on the wrong end of a lawsuit. It is illegal to retaliate against an employee for complaining about discrimination or another violation of a workplace law to you, someone else in your company, or a government agency.

This does not mean that you can't give an employee who complains or supports another employee's complaint a negative performance evaluation if the employee's job performance warrants it. It does mean, however, that you must be extra prepared to back up your negative evaluation with documents and evidence in case the employee claims that your real motive was to retaliate for the complaint.

Don't Forget to Document

This book suggests procedures that will ensure you document an employee's performance throughout the year. If you follow these procedures, you will have documentation to back up everything you say in the performance evaluation. This is very important, because you may want to use your performance evaluation as evidence in your favor if you become embroiled in an employee lawsuit—and the evaluation will only be as good as the documentation on which it is based.

In addition, documentation can help you counter claims of bias. For example, imagine that you evaluate an employee negatively on productivity, and the employee claims that you did so because of racial bias. You have documents that show that the employee's sales dropped significantly in the past year and that the employee has the worst sales record in your department. Your documentation provides proof that your opinion is based on objective, job-related facts, not discriminatory bias.

Checklist: Avoiding Legal Trouble. Use the following checklist to make sure you've avoided the legal traps covered in this chapter. You'll also find a copy of the checklist in Appendix B and on the CD-ROM at the back of this book.

☑ Checklist:
Avoiding Legal Trouble

As you put the finishing touches on a performance appraisal, review the following statements. If you cannot say any of them with certainty, then you may have stepped into a legal trap. In that case, reread the section of this chapter that pertains to the issue.

In this performance evaluation:

☐ I do not make any predictions about the employee's future at this company.

☐ I do not promise the employee continued employment.

☐ I do not reassure the employee that his or her job is secure.

☐ I do not predict how likely it is that the employee will receive a promotion.

☐ I have not limited or softened my criticism of the employee's performance to be nice or to avoid conflict.

☐ I have not left out any issues because I don't want to confront the employee about them.

☐ I have not tried to spare the employee's feelings by ignoring or down-playing problems.

☐ I was able to thoroughly review this employee's performance, so the evaluation is comprehensive.

☐ If I am thinking that I may have to fire the employee someday, I have reflected the reasons behind such thoughts.

☐ I do not use slurs or potentially offensive language.

☐ I do not make any sexual comments.

☐ I do not make jokes.

☐ I do not say or imply anything that criticizes the employee for being different from others (for example, the employee "doesn't fit in") unless I have specifically related it to job performance.

☐ If the employee has one or more protected characteristics, I have not mentioned the characteristic(s).

☐ I have not based my evaluation on any stereotypes I might have about the employee based on the employee's protected characteristic(s).

☐ All of the feedback I have included is specific and related to the employee's job.

☐ If the employee has a physical or mental impairment, I have consulted with either human resources or the company's legal counsel before completing this evaluation.

☐ If the employee has complained about discrimination, harassment, or another violation of workplace law, or supported another employee's complaint, I have been very careful to document any negative feedback I have included. I have evaluated the employee fairly and have not given negative feedback just to get back at the employee for complaining.

☐ If I were questioned about anything I have included in this evaluation, I could support my statements with documents or other evidence.

Test Your Knowledge

Questions

1. All employees are at-will employees. □ True □ False

2. I can fire at-will employees for any reason. □ True □ False

3. The only way to form a contract with an employee is through a written document signed by the employee and the CEO. □ True □ False

4. Nothing I say in a performance appraisal can destroy an at-will employment relationship. □ True □ False

5. It's legal to reassure employees that their jobs are secure. □ True □ False

6. If I want to terminate an employee, the fact that my reasons are not reflected in the employee's performance evaluations may hurt my company if the employee sues. □ True □ False

7. Performance evaluations can't be used as evidence in an employee's wrongful termination lawsuit against my company. □ True □ False

8. Offensive words alone—without some other discriminatory action—cannot get me into legal trouble. □ True □ False

9. If an employee's physical or mental impairment is preventing the employee from performing well, it's the employee's problem, not mine. □ True □ False

10. I cannot use the performance evaluation process as a way of getting back at employees who complain about me. □ True □ False

Answers

1. **False.** Employees who have an employment contract stating that they can only be fired for just cause are not at-will employees. Although you can create the contract with a formal document, you can also create it just through the things that you say to the employee.

2. **False.** You can fire at-will employees for any reason that isn't illegal. Terminating someone because of a protected characteristic (for example, race, gender, national origin, religion, age, or disability) is illegal, as is terminating someone for complaining about illegal conduct.

3. **False.** A member of management can create a contract with an employee through spoken promises or assurances or through statements made to the employee in a performance evaluation.

4. **False.** If, in a performance evaluation, you make promises or give assurances about an employee's job security or future at the company, you can destroy the at-will employment relationship.

5. **True.** It's certainly legal to reassure employees—but you'd better mean it, because some courts may view those assurances as binding contracts.

6. **True.** A wise manager makes sure that all performance problems are reflected in a performance evaluation so that, if the time comes to fire the employee, the problems have been documented and the reasoning is there.

7. **False.** Performance evaluations are often the key evidence in a wrongful termination lawsuit.

8. **False.** Harassment is a form of discrimination; if your words are offensive enough, they alone could form the basis of a discrimination lawsuit.

9. **False.** If you know that an employee's disability is posing an obstacle, and if you can make a reasonable accommodation, then you are legally required to do so.

10. **True.** The law prohibits you from retaliating against employees for complaining about violations of workplace law, including discrimination.

■

Chapter 3

Performance Objectives

Chapter Highlights

- Developing performance objectives for an employee is a collaborative process between the employee and you. Together, you and the employee decide on the objectives the employee will strive for during the appraisal period (which is usually one year).

- Job requirements describe what an employee in a particular job should accomplish and how the employee should perform that work.

- Job requirements should apply to a job regardless of who is performing it.

- Identify job requirements before the employee starts the job. Communicate expected job requirements to the employee and solicit feedback on existing job requirements from the employee at each year-end evaluation meeting. (For new employees, convey job requirements in a meeting within the employee's first three months.)

- Goals describe things that you and the employee would like the employee to accomplish beyond the job requirements.

- Tailor goals to each employee as an individual, based on the employee's strengths and weaknesses.

- Make goals reasonable, realistic, challenging, specific, measurable (if possible), related to the job, and consistent with your company's core values and strategic plan.

- Help employees prioritize their performance objectives.

- Heaping too many performance objectives onto an employee can actually diminish performance, not improve it.

- Don't make promises to employees about what will happen if they perform well. If you do, you could create an implied contract, destroying the employee's at-will employment status.

- When setting goals, don't try to change an employee's personality. Focus on what your employees do, not who they are.

- Don't stereotype employees when identifying their goals.

- If a goal is new or outside of the ordinary tasks that the employee does, help the employee figure out how to meet it by creating an action plan.

- Write performance objectives in a formal document. Use concrete details, be specific, and use active (rather than passive) verbs.

T he foundation of any performance evaluation system is a set of performance objectives in which you identify what your company and you expect of an employee. Individualized performance objectives give employees something to strive for—a target on the horizon to always keep in sight. As the year progresses, employees can refine and adjust their work to make sure they are on track with their objectives. You may even find that, with well-defined performance objectives, employees will exceed your (and their) expectations.

In your company's performance appraisal system, objectives may be called any number of things: responsibilities, accountabilities, duties, results, outputs, targets, and so on. Regardless of what you call them, however, all performance objectives are essentially the same thing: a way to define what you expect from an employee and measure how well the employee meets those expectations. This book uses the terms "requirements" and "goals" when referring to an employee's performance objectives, but the guidelines it presents will be useful to you no matter what terms your company uses.

A surprising number of employees are in the dark about the performance objectives for their jobs. For example, the November/December 2005 issue of *Compensation and Benefits Review* states that roughly half of those responding to a recent survey claimed that they did not know what their supervisors expected of them. But research has shown that setting effective performance objectives is invaluable for improving employee performance. It can also lead to higher job satisfaction and greater respect for the appraisal process among employees. Why such results? Because setting clear objectives clues employees in to what their companies expect of them. Employees who don't understand this fundamental element of their jobs are left confused, insecure, and aimless. In contrast, employees who know what to strive for can focus their efforts, pay attention to critical tasks, and avoid distractions. As a result, they have increased confidence in their abilities, higher morale, and better job performance.

This chapter focuses on how to identify performance objectives—or job requirements and goals—and how to write these objectives up as an employee's performance plan.

When You Work in a Multinational Corporation

The ordinary challenges of setting performance objectives are compounded when you work in a different country from an employee you are responsible for reviewing. After all, the job exists in a context that you may not have a chance to personally observe or that you may not fully comprehend. There may be language barriers that make it tough for you to discuss the job with the employee's coworkers, vendors, and customers. There may be logistical problems with gathering the necessary documents from overseas.

Some multinational companies are aware of these issues; some are not. The most important thing, however, is that you be aware of them and take as many steps as possible to ensure that you set reasonable and appropriate objectives despite these potential hurdles. Talk to the employee about the issue; get advice from other managers who are in the same situation; and see if your human resources department can help.

Identifying Job Requirements

A job requirement is a description of what you want an employee in a particular position to accomplish and how you want an employee in that job to perform. Every employee who holds a job should meet essentially the same requirements for that job. In other words, the requirements reflect the features of the position, irrespective of the abilities or skills of the particular employee who fills it at any given time. A set of requirements for a particular job will look very much like the job description for that job. In fact, the job description you wrote when advertising for the position is one of the best resources you have when identifying that job's requirements.

Types of Job Requirements

There are two kinds of job requirements: result requirements and behavior requirements.

- A result requirement is a concrete description of a result that you expect any employee who holds a particular job to achieve. For example, a result requirement for newspaper reporters might be to write three stories a

week; for proofreaders, to miss no more than one error per story; for a
salesperson, to make $10,000 in sales each quarter.

- A behavior requirement is a description of how you want any employee
  in a particular job to behave while getting that job done. Often, behavior
  requirements reflect your company's values. For example, your company
  might place a high value on customer service. You might, therefore, set
  a behavior requirement for all salespeople to answer customer questions
  cheerfully and respectfully.

Because job requirements remain consistent for a position regardless of who
holds that position, you should identify job requirements before employees
start their jobs. Then—because a given job may change over time based on the
company's needs, strategic plan, and so on—you and the employee together
should reevaluate and adjust these requirements at the year-end evaluation
meeting. (See Chapter 6 for more about this meeting.)

Resources for Identifying Job Requirements

To identify the requirements for a particular job, look at how the job fits within
your business. What is a person who holds this job responsible for? What are the
essential tasks you need a person in this job to accomplish? What is the purpose
of the job? Historically, what have employees in the job been able to accomplish?

Start with old performance evaluations for the position. Has a previous
manager done some legwork and identified useful job requirements? Do you
see themes in both the positive and negative comments about employees who
previously held the position that tell you what the jobholder must accomplish?

Review the job description for the position. It should identify the requirements
for the job and let you know what people in your company expect from the
jobholder.

If you must write a job description. *The Job Description Handbook* by
Margie Mader-Clark (Nolo) contains checklists, worksheets, resources,
sample language, and step-by-step instructions—all designed to help you write an
effective job description.

Look at your company's mission and values statements. The job requirements
for every position on your team should dovetail with these core descriptions of
the qualities your company holds in high esteem and the goals your company has
identified for itself.

Other places where you can look for useful information are the resumes of previous jobholders and notes from exit interviews of previous jobholders. In addition, talk to coworkers, customers, and vendors who interact with the jobholder, to find out what they need from the person in this position.

Employees themselves—both employees who hold or have held the job and employees who interact with and depend upon the jobholder—can be a valuable resource for defining requirements for a particular job. For example, when defining a vehicle dispatcher's job, you could learn from the vehicle drivers that they need a dispatcher to be able to give clear and concise directions. Other dispatchers themselves might not realize how important this behavior is.

Job Requirements Must Be Job-Related

Choose only requirements that are truly related to the job—meaning they are actually necessary to the position itself. This is important for both practical and legal reasons.

Practically, it does neither the employee nor you any good to force the employee to live up to a requirement that doesn't help your company. For example, requiring chefs to be friendly to customers makes no sense if they have no contact with customers—and requiring chefs to meet this requirement could detract from their more important function of preparing meals.

Legally, you are not justified in punishing an employee for failing to meet a requirement that is not actually required by or related to the position that the employee holds. Disciplining, demoting, or terminating an employee for failing to meet a requirement that is not job-related does not constitute just cause. (See Chapter 2 for a discussion of just cause.)

Job Requirements Must Be Specific

The more specific a job requirement is, the easier it will be for an employee to meet. Companies often make the mistake of using vague language to describe how they want a job to be performed. For example, you might say you want anyone in the position of account representative to "take initiative" or "be self-starting." But what do these terms really mean? To be useful, the requirement should help the employee understand what you really expect. If a job requirement leaves room for the employee and you to disagree about what's expected, it will be difficult to decide whether the employee has met the requirement.

To guard against vagueness, focus on the actions you want the employee to take, not on the character trait or personality type you want the employee to have. For example, instead of setting "take initiative" as a job requirement, spell out how you expect an employee to act or what you expect the employee to do. Do you want the employee to create his or her own product ideas? Do you want the employee to develop personal sales contacts? Do you want the employee to implement his or her own ways to attract clients? When you focus on actions instead of traits, you give the employee a greater understanding of what you expect, while giving yourself a more concrete standard against which to measure the employee's performance.

Checklist: Identifying Job Requirements. Use the following checklist to make sure you've consulted every available resource when developing the job requirements for a position. You'll also find a copy of the checklist in Appendix B and on the CD-ROM at the back of this book.

☑ Checklist:
Identifying Job Requirements

Here is a list of resources to consult when identifying job requirements:

- ☐ Your company's core values as evidenced in its strategic plan, mission statement, and values statements.

- ☐ The job description.

- ☐ Interviews with the employee who currently holds the job.

- ☐ Past evaluations for employees who held the position.

- ☐ Resumes of top performers in the position.

- ☐ Exit interviews with people who held the job.

- ☐ Interviews with coworkers, customers, and vendors who interact with the jobholder.

Identifying Goals

The second measure by which you will evaluate your employees is through developmental goals. These goals are tailored to each employee as an individual, depending on the employee's strengths, weaknesses, and experiences. Goals are different from requirements because they are about the employee as an individual—in other words, you focus on what makes sense for this person, rather than for this job. As a result, performance goals will not be the same for all employees in the same job category (but job requirements will).

Together, you and the employee will choose goals based on:

- weak spots you see in the employee's overall performance that you'd like the employee to improve upon
- strengths and abilities that you'd like the employee to nurture and develop, and
- skills that the employee can learn that will improve job performance.

For example, a store manager might do a great job overseeing the day-to-day operations of the store but have weak writing skills that make his reports impossible to understand. One job requirement for the employee's position is to write readable reports. A developmental goal for the employee would be to take a writing course at a local community college.

Or, your best salesperson might have a number of Spanish-speaking customers in her territory. A job requirement for that position is to increase sales. You and the salesperson decide that speaking Spanish would improve sales among the Spanish-speaking population. A developmental goal for the salesperson would be to complete a conversational Spanish course by the end of the year.

Set Goals With the Employee

Collaboration is the key to successful goal setting. If the employee helps to create the goals, chances are that he or she will genuinely want to meet them. Working with an employee to develop goals will also give you the benefit of the employee's knowledge: Employees often recognize their own strengths and weaknesses better than you do—and understand their jobs in ways you haven't considered. It's important to include their ideas on where and how they can improve their performance.

In addition, research has shown that employees and managers together set more challenging goals than managers alone. You may not feel comfortable asking an employee to make a stretch that the employee in fact wants to make. Also, employees are more likely to meet goals they have helped create than goals that managers set on their own.

To do this, meet with each employee formally to discuss and set goals. For a new employee, schedule a goal-setting meeting in the first few weeks of employment so that the employee has goals to work toward during the first year. Also at that meeting, tell the employee about the job requirements for his or her position and give some informal feedback on any work that the employee has already done for you. For current employees, set and reevaluate goals in each appraisal period, during each year-end evaluation. (See Chapter 6 for a discussion of the year-end evaluation.)

Before you meet with an employee to set goals, encourage the employee to prepare by thinking about how to improve his or her current abilities and whether there are skills he or she would like to acquire that could contribute to improving performance in the current job. Provide the employee with relevant information about the company's core values and/or strategic plan and any specific goals or plans you have for your department. Give the employee information about your company's current position and future plans, if appropriate. Explain that you want to identify individual goals for the employee to strive for—both for the benefit of the company and for the employee's own career development. At the meeting, discuss and choose the employee's goals for the next year with the employee.

After you have identified the employee's goals for the upcoming year, find out what, if anything, the employee needs from you to meet the goals. To the extent that the goal requires money or time, the company should consider providing it.

For example, in order for an instructor to teach more-advanced classes, he or she may need to attend a continuing education course, which you should consider having the company pay for. Or, if you set a goal with an account representative to take on more-complicated or bigger accounts, you may need to provide additional support staff to help the representative reach the goal.

Checklist: Preparing an Employe for Goal Setting. Before you meet with an employee to set goals, use the following checklist to make sure you've provided all necessary information. You'll also find a copy of the checklist in Appendix B and on the CD-ROM at the back of this book.

☑ Checklist:
Preparing an Employee for Goal Setting

Before your goal-setting session with an employee (either in an initial meeting or at each year-end evaluation meeting), make sure that you:

☐ Provide a copy of your company's strategic plan and/or core values.

☐ If your company has made projections about the future that are relevant to the employee's job, provide those.

☐ Provide a current job description for the employee's position.

☐ For current employees, provide a copy of the employee's performance evaluation from the previous year.

☐ Ask the employee to make a list of professional development goals:

☐ What training would the employee like?

☐ What skills would the employee like to acquire or hone?

☐ What new tasks or responsibilities would the employee like to take on?

Guidelines for Effective Goal Setting

This section provides some overall guidelines to follow when identifying performance goals with an employee.

Get SMART

A common acronym that human resources professionals use when defining objectives is SMART:

- **S**pecific: The goal must be well defined and understood.
- **M**easurable: You and the employee must have some way of determining whether the employee met the goal.
- **A**pplicable: The goal must fit within the company's strategic plan.
- **R**elevant: The goal must make sense in terms of what the employee and the department are trying to accomplish.
- **T**ime bound: There must be a time limit on how long the employee has to accomplish the goal.

Don't Be Excessive

In your year-end evaluation meeting (or in an initial objective-setting meeting, for new employees), you should spend time brainstorming with the employee to come up with goals for the coming year. In doing so, you will probably develop a long wish list of things you would like the employee to accomplish. After all, a brainstorming session should be creative and inclusive. Devising an all-inclusive list is helpful, as long as you then whittle the list down to the employee's essential goals. If you fail to limit this list to a reasonable number, your employee won't be able to focus and will feel overwhelmed.

Some managers think, incorrectly, that the more performance goals, the better. On the contrary, you can actually lower employee performance by heaping too many goals (and requirements, for that matter) onto an employee's back. Feeling unable to accomplish any one thing can diminish employee performance, while being able to accomplish a few important goals well can motivate an employee and keep morale high.

Be Realistic About Abilities

You may have lofty ideas about what you want an employee to accomplish in the coming year, but if the performance goals you establish are out of reach for the employee, you are setting the employee up for failure. Not only is this unfair, it also risks turning a good employee into a problem employee who is unhappy and demoralized.

Of course, you can and should ask an employee to perform at a certain basic level (that's what the job requirements discussed above are all about). And if the employee can't perform at that basic level, then you need to do something about it—whether through training or reassignment or discipline.

But in the context of goals, you have a lot of leeway in what you ask of an employee—both in terms of the difficulty of the goal and the type. Use that leeway to tailor goals to employees and the unique contribution that they can make to your team and your company. Be aware of your employees' skills and abilities and develop a sense of what is a good stretch for them as opposed to what is simply beyond them. Be honest with yourself about the amount of support and resources that your company and you can provide.

When identifying goals for an employee, ask these questions:

- Does the employee have the education and training necessary to accomplish this task?
- Has the employee demonstrated the skills necessary to accomplish this task?
- Is the company providing the resources necessary to support the employee in accomplishing this task?
- Does the employee have control over the people and circumstances necessary to accomplish the task?
- Given the other items in the employee's performance plan, does the employee have the time to accomplish this task?

If your answer to any of these questions is "no," then you should reconsider whether the goal is appropriate. If providing training or committing more resources to the employee will change your answer, then the goal might be appropriate. If not, it's neither fair nor effective to keep the goal on the list hoping that the employee will somehow manage to overcome the obstacles to achievement.

Be Appropriately Challenging

Although you shouldn't set unreachable goals, don't make things too simple for your employees, either. Research has shown that having challenging goals leads to better performance. Employees like to stretch and learn new things. They feel valued and needed when they are given greater responsibilities, which can shore up their confidence and, in turn, improve their performance. Also, your company will grow if your employees do a little more and a little better each year. When setting goals, challenge your employees and ask them to venture out of their comfort zone. As long as the objectives you pick are reasonable and realistic, a challenge will be good for the employee and your company as a whole.

Be Specific

Research has shown that specific performance measures lead to better performance than do vague statements such as "work harder" and "do your best." The more concrete and clear a performance objective, the easier it is for an employee to meet. Use details like numbers and dates. Use action verbs. For more about how to be specific when writing performance objectives, see "Writing Requirements and Goals," below.

Choose Job-Related Goals

However laudable a goal is in general, it must be firmly related to the employee's job. Although job goals are individual, they are not personal: They must relate both to the employee's professional development and to the employee's role within the company. Otherwise, at best you'll be wasting time, energy, and money on skills that the employee will not use to help the company, and, at worst, you'll be courting legal trouble. To be legally safe in basing an employment decision on an employee's ability or inability to meet a goal, that goal must be job-related.

Set Measurable Goals

If possible, you should be able to measure whether the employee has met a goal. If you can identify a fair way to measure the goal, you will minimize the risk that the employee and you will disagree over whether the employee actually accomplished it.

For example, if you set a goal for a salesperson to increase the amount of money he or she brings in by 20 percent in a year, determining whether the salesperson accomplished the goal is easy and measurable: Simply review the sales records and do the math. But if, instead, you set a goal for the employee to "be a more effective salesperson," you may disagree over what "effective" means. The employee might consider the type or quality of sales, while you might be interested solely in increasing the number of customers.

Of course, not all jobs and not all objectives lend themselves to measurement. It's okay to have requirements and goals that aren't easily measured—just try to keep them to a minimum. And, be especially specific when writing them. (See "Writing Requirements and Goals," below, for tips.)

Create an Action Plan

If the performance goal is particularly complicated or unusual, the employee might have trouble figuring out how to go about achieving it. If that is the case, you and the employee can create an action plan together. This way, you and the employee will know how the employee plans to meet the goals and what support the employee will get from the company and you. For example, will the employee need additional training? Do you need to provide new tools or personnel? How will the employee find the time to do the work? Answering these types of questions at the outset can help the employee achieve the goal—which means that everyone wins.

Avoid Personality Issues

Beware of trying to change an employee's personality traits through performance goals. For example, if you want an employee to improve relations with coworkers, and the employee is particularly shy or is uncomfortable in social situations, it's not a valid goal to have the employee attend more social functions. Rather, think of another way for the employee to improve coworker relations—perhaps through working on more committees. Trying to change someone's personality is rarely possible, and it sets both you and the employee up for failure. You can use goals to help employees change what they do, but not who they are.

Avoid Stereotypes

It may be natural to make assumptions about a person based on characteristics such as race, national origin, age, or gender, but it's also illegal. (See Chapter 2 for more about stereotypes and illegal discrimination.) When identifying performance goals for an employee, do not stereotype. Do not assume, for example, that it's not an appropriate goal for a female employee to learn how to fix machinery. Base your ideas on the employee as an individual. Use what you know—not what you assume—to guide you in finding appropriate performance measures.

Don't Make Promises

When setting performance goals, be careful not to make promises or guarantees regarding what will happen if the employee achieves the objectives. For example, don't tell an employee that accomplishing a task will lead to a promotion, because the employee may construe this as a promise—and could argue that you created a legally binding contract. If you make an employment-related promise you don't keep, you might end up on the unpleasant end of an employee's breach of contract lawsuit. (See Chapter 2 for more about this issue.)

Checklist: Identify Goals. Use the following checklist to make sure the goals you and the employee set are appropriate and effective. You'll also find a copy of the checklist in Appendix B and on the CD-ROM at the back of this book.

☑ Checklist: Identifying Goals

When identifying performance goals, make sure each one meets the following criteria:

- ☐ It is consistent with company goals.

- ☐ It is reasonable and realistic.

- ☐ It is challenging but within the employee's reach.

- ☐ It is specific.

- ☐ It is related to the employee's job.

- ☐ It is measurable or, if it cannot be measured, it is especially specific.

- ☐ If necessary, it has an action plan attached.

- ☐ It does not try to change the employee's personality.

- ☐ It is not based on assumptions or stereotypes.

- ☐ It does not promise the employee something now or in the future.

When to Set Performance Objectives

For current employees, discuss requirements and goals during each year-end evaluation meeting. (See Chapter 6 for a discussion of the year-end evaluation and the goal-setting process.) For new employees, have an initial meeting earlier, ideally within the first three months of employment, to set out requirements and goals for the employee's first year. At the end of each yearly appraisal period, the employee and you will use these requirements and goals to assess how well the employee has done over the past year and to create a new performance plan for the coming year.

Writing Requirements and Goals

For job requirements and goals to be useful, you must write them down in a formal document. While you evaluate and coach the employee throughout the year (a process discussed in Chapter 4), you will refer to this document to assess the employee's performance and keep the employee on track. Then, at the year-end evaluation, you will evaluate the employee's performance based largely on this document. The essential question your evaluation will answer is: Did the employee's performance live up to these requirements and goals?

Because job requirements and goals are so important, you should write them so that anyone reading them can understand what they mean. Here are some tips for writing requirements and goals clearly:

- Be specific. For example, don't include phrases such as "work harder" or "improve quality." Rather, give specifics such as "increase sales by 20 percent over last year."
- Focus on what you want the employee to do, not on who you want the employee to be. For instance, don't say "be a friendlier person." Instead, say "reduce customer and coworker complaints."
- Use concrete details, such as names, numbers, and dates.
- Use active verbs, not passive verbs, which will underscore your expectation that the employee, not some disembodied force, is the individual who has to perform. For example, don't say "deadlines will be met." Rather, say "John will meet 75% of his deadlines this quarter."
- If appropriate, state the date by which you want the employee to achieve the requirement.
- If the objective is measurable, describe how and when you will measure it.
- Unless it is obvious, describe how the requirement or goal relates to the job.

The classic recipe for writing a performance objective is the following:

[Name of employee] will [verb] [description] by [deadline].

So, for example,

[John] will [wash] [the outside of the car] by [4 p.m. today].

Once you have written requirements for the job and goals for the employee, prioritize the entries within each category, ranking them from most to least important. With a prioritized list, the employee will know how to allocate time and energy among the various requirements and goals. If the employee can't get through the entire list by the time the next review rolls around, the employee should have at least addressed the most important requirements and goals. Note, however, that you should only include a reasonable number of requirements and goals, so that the employee does not feel overwhelmed.

EXAMPLES OF HOW TO PHRASE JOB REQUIREMENTS:

Bad: Answer a sufficient number of customer service hotline calls.

Good: The employee will answer a weekly average of 10 customer service hotline calls per shift.

Bad: Edit quickly.

Good: The employee will edit a weekly average of 120 inches of copy per shift.

Bad: Be self-motivated.

Good: The employee will generate and develop his or her own customer base. At least half of the new accounts should be accounts the employee develops.

EXAMPLE OF HOW TO PHRASE GOALS:

Bad: Andy will improve his plant transplant technique.

Good: Andy will observe senior nursery personnel when they perform difficult transplants. He will study *Western Gardening*'s chapter on transplants and will take responsibility for at least ten transplants per week by April, 20xx. By September, 20xx, he will perform at least 15 transplants per week, of which at least 12 are successful.

Checklist: Writing Performance Objectives. Use the following checklist to make sure the performance objectives you develop with an employee are effective and appropriate. You'll also find a copy of the checklist in Appendix B and on the CD-ROM at the back of this book.

☑ Checklist: Writing Performance Objectives

When you write up a performance objective—be it a job requirement or a goal—make sure it meets these criteria:

- ☐ It is specific, not general.

- ☐ It describes what the employee should do, not who the employee should be.

- ☐ It contains concrete details.

- ☐ It uses active verbs, not passive verbs.

- ☐ If the requirement or goal is measurable, it describes how it will be measured.

- ☐ If appropriate, it gives a deadline for completion.

- ☐ Unless it is obvious, the objective describes how it relates to the job.

Test Your Knowledge

Questions

1. Although company goals are relevant when choosing performance objectives for an employee, they aren't a significant consideration.   ☐ True ☐ False

2. Giving an employee as many performance objectives as you can think of may diminish employee performance.   ☐ True ☐ False

3. You should set only easy goals. Do not ask an employee to do something new or stretch beyond what he or she has done in the past.   ☐ True ☐ False

4. If you cannot measure a performance objective, you should not use it.   ☐ True ☐ False

5. Your responsibility is to identify the employee's job requirements and goals. The employee's responsibility is to figure out how to accomplish them.   ☐ True ☐ False

6. Job requirements are individual to the employee.   ☐ True ☐ False

7. Employees cannot help identify job requirements.   ☐ True ☐ False

8. When setting performance objectives, you should be concerned about the employee's professional growth and development.   ☐ True ☐ False

9. A company's strategic plan should be kept secret so that competitors can't discover it. Your employees do not need to know about it as long as they do as they are told.   ☐ True ☐ False

10. It's part of the employee's job to figure out which job requirements and goals are most important. The employee, not the manager, should be prioritizing.   ☐ True ☐ False

Answers

1. **False.** Company goals are more than relevant; they are a very important consideration when setting requirements and goals for your employees. Everything you ask your employees to do should serve those goals.

2. **True.** If you ask your employees to do too much, not only will they be unable to do everything you ask, but they may even do less than if you had given them a realistic number of tasks in the first place. Assigning too much can be overwhelming and can lower performance instead of improving it.

3. **False.** Although you want to be realistic, it is important that you challenge your employees. The goals you set should force them to stretch a little.

4. **False.** It is nice to have measurable requirements and goals, but not everything an employee does will lend itself to objective measurement. If you know you won't be able to measure a requirement or goal, be especially specific in describing it.

5. **False.** A manager should work with the employee to review the job's requirements and set the employee's goals. Also, part of a manager's job is to help the employee develop an action plan for complicated requirements and goals.

6. **False.** Job requirements are tied to the job, not to the employee holding the job.

7. **False.** Employees will often be your best resource in identifying or reevaluating the requirements for a particular job.

8. **True.** An employee's professional growth and development are key concerns when setting job goals—as long as the goals are also job related and dovetail with company values and plans.

9. **False.** The only way employees can help a company achieve its strategic plan is for them to know about the plan. Sharing your strategic plan with employees (which you can do confidentially) is also a good way to ensure that the requirements and goals an employee and you set relate to that plan.

10. **False.** You must help the employee prioritize the requirements and goals. Otherwise, you run the risk of the employee spending too much time on unimportant objectives and not enough on important ones.

Chapter 4

Observation and Documentation

Chapter Highlights

- For a performance evaluation system to be effective, you must observe and document employee performance throughout the year, as it happens.

- Most of the documenting you do can be informal and brief; it doesn't have to take a lot of time. As a bonus, it will save you time when you conduct the formal evaluation.

- Documenting employee performance as it happens also increases the fairness of your interim and year-end appraisals. Having documentation spanning the entire appraisal period ensures that you will base the evaluation on the employee's performance throughout the year, not just the most recent events or the ones that happen to stick out in your memory.

- Managers must develop first-hand knowledge of employee performance through actively observing their employees on the job.

- To keep track of employee performance as it happens, keep an informal performance log on each employee in your own files.

- In the performance log, don't make an entry for every day that an employee shows up to work. Just document noteworthy events, both good and bad.

- Often, day-to-day feedback can happen quickly and casually. If you see a problem happening, address it orally in the moment, then record it in a log and/or follow up with an email. Often, you can nip problems in the bud this way.

- In addition to the performance log and casual communication, give employees written notes when they perform well and when they perform poorly. This book calls these notes "kudos" and "ticklers," but you can use any terms you like. These notes add to your ongoing documentation and provide feedback to your employees.

- Kudos are short notes that let employees know that you notice and appreciate their efforts; they do not have to be elaborate.

- Ticklers are notes you use to coach and counsel an employee. Use them to give employees feedback or advice. Like kudos, ticklers do not have to be elaborate.

To make your performance evaluation system effective and easy to manage, you should observe and document employee performance on an ongoing basis. Pay attention to your employees and their performance throughout the year, not just in the days preceding an evaluation meeting. When you observe something—either good or bad—record your observation at the time instead of waiting until you write the evaluation.

Most of your record keeping can be informal and brief—it doesn't have to eat up too much of your time. And, any time it takes will be well spent. When you evaluate an employee formally, you will have already done most of the work, having amassed a record of the employee's performance for the entire year (or whatever time period your review covers). Instead of racking your memory for examples of the employee's good or bad performance or trying to reconstruct events, you can simply review your notes.

Documenting employee performance as it happens also increases the fairness of your interim and year-end appraisals. Having documentation ensures that you will base the evaluation on the employee's entire performance, not just the most recent events or the ones that happen to stick out in your memory. And, if you ever have to justify in a lawsuit any negative actions you have taken against an employee, you'll be more successful if you can point to a careful and complete paper trail.

A surprising number of companies do not provide guidance on documentation, leaving it up to each manager to figure out how and when to write things down. No matter what system your company uses—or even if it uses no system at all—this chapter will be useful to you: It provides practical and legal rules for documenting employee performance that apply in any context.

This chapter describes how you can document employee performance completely throughout the year by using three simple tools:

- performance logs—your own personal record of what employees have done (or failed to do) throughout the year
- kudos—notes that you give (or emails that you send) to employees to recognize exceptionally good performance, and
- ticklers—notes that you give (or emails that you send) to employees to alert them that they have veered off track and need to improve their performance.

Establish a system for ongoing communication. This book uses the terms "kudos" and "ticklers" to describe written feedback you provide to your employees. You can use any term you like to refer to these types of notes—just use some system of ongoing communication and documentation.

Informal communication is okay. The system of kudos and ticklers this chapter describes is a formal one for documenting and giving feedback. This system should not take the place of informal day-to-day communication in the workplace. If you see a problem happening and it feels natural and appropriate to address it orally in the moment, then do so. This is often the best way to nip performance problems in the bud, so you don't have to get to the level of ticklers and warnings. But be sure to either follow up with an email or make a note on your calendar or in a performance log so that you have documentation of what happened.

Don't make up documentation after the fact. A company that fails to document employee performance regularly may be tempted to do so later, when it is sued by an employee who was disciplined or fired. It's perfectly okay to write down your impressions of how an employee performed, even if some time has passed since the incidents you're describing, but it's not okay to attempt to pass off these writings as having been made earlier. A judge or jury that learns of your dishonest attempts to re-create a past record will disregard your false documentation and doubt your credibility.

Observing Your Employees

Before you can evaluate an employee's performance, you must witness that performance first-hand. Although this should go without saying, it doesn't: Too many managers aren't aware of what is going on under their very noses. When it comes to evaluating your employees' performance, it's not enough to sit in your office or behind a desk and let your employees work at a distance. Unless you personally observe your employees in action, you will have to rely entirely on secondary sources—such as sales reports and feedback from coworkers or customers—to assess how your employees have performed. Of course, input from secondary sources is important, but a manager who relies solely on them is missing half the story.

If you want to know what is going on in your department—who is doing what and how well—get out of your office and become part of the working life of your employees. One researcher called this technique "management by walking around"—an apt term. This doesn't mean that you have to micromanage or be overbearing; it just means that you should be aware of your employees' efforts.

As you go about your day, pay attention to what is happening around you. Don't focus solely on results; understand the story behind those results. Circulate among your employees—walk out onto the floor or into the showroom. Check in with employees on their workloads and work progress. Have an open-door policy for employee complaints and feedback.

When something noteworthy happens—either positive or negative—take the time to analyze the reasons behind the event. If an employee missed a deadline, was it solely the employee's fault? Or were other factors at play, such as tardy supplies, uncooperative coworkers, or miscommunication? If a particular project is a great success, figure out what worked and how you can help your employees replicate the good results. Engaging in this type of analysis is an important part of observing your employees' performance.

If you are in a multinational corporation and must appraise an employee who works overseas, it won't be possible to actually observe employee performance. The same is true in situations where employees work off site (perhaps at home or on the road) or work at different times than you (for example, on a flex-time schedule). In situations such as these, you can still be aware of employee performance by doing things such as monitoring data; reviewing work product; and checking in with vendors, customers, and coworkers on a fairly regular basis. Talk to or email these employees frequently as well; regular communication with these employees is almost more important than with employees who work right outside your door. Be open about the challenge of managing someone who is not on site. Ask them for help in understanding what they are doing. In the case of employee who work overseas, try to make room in your budget for a visit to the employee's work site, even if you can go only once a year.

Maintaining a Performance Log

The best way to document an employee's performance is to keep a running list of events or incidents. A useful tool for doing this is an informal performance log that you keep—either in a paper file, a computer file, or a notebook—on each employee you supervise. When the employee does something noteworthy, either good or bad, take a moment to jot it down in the log. A performance log helps you keep track of the employee's performance in a format that will be useful to you when you evaluate the employee formally at the end of the appraisal period. It should not be an exhaustive daily log of everything the employee does or does not do.

This section explains what to put in the log and how to format it.

Email is okay. In today's workplace, many managers keep track of events by emailing themselves or their workers and then saving a copy of the email, in either a computer or a paper file. If that's how you keep track of employee performance, that's fine. There are, as they say, many ways to skin a cat. If you prefer using email to keeping a performance log, then by all means do so. Just be sure that your emails follow the guidelines suggested in this section.

What to Include

Include only noteworthy events in your log. This means that you should not make an entry for every day that the employee shows up for work. Include only those incidents that are out of the ordinary, stand out as markers of the employee's performance, or are contrary to your company rules or procedures. For example, you might note when a worker shows up late, makes a significant mistake, or makes an extra effort to meet a deadline.

The majority of entries will relate to the requirements and goals that you and the employee set. In addition, there may be times when the employee does something noteworthy outside the context of requirements and goals that you should include. Use the log to keep track of comments, compliments, or complaints that you receive about an employee—but ignore rumors and gossip. If you receive these comments via email, then you can simply save a copy of the email rather than adding an entry to the log. Just be sure that you have a system that ensures you don't forget about these emails when it is time to evaluate the employee.

If you are documenting an employee's poor performance or a negative event, include any information you have that could explain what happened. For example, if an employee's sales are lower than expected, it would be useful to note that sales for the entire market sector are also low and that perhaps the lackluster performance is due to something beyond the employee's control, such as a poor economy. Identifying the reasons behind an employee's poor performance or bad conduct is an important first step to helping the employee develop strategies to improve.

Once you begin keeping track of negative incidents, you must be consistent. If a judge or jury reviews your performance log during a lawsuit and there is no entry for a date the employee worked, they will assume that the employee performed at an acceptable level for that day—no better, no worse. This means that if you include some entries about an employee's negative performance, you'll have a tough time trying to raise additional negative incidents that you did not include in the log. To be believed, you'll have to explain why you didn't follow your own system of note taking—and why a judge or jury should credit your current version of events over an empty spot in your log.

How to Write an Entry

Because a performance log is a tool for you to use when you sit down to evaluate an employee, you should keep it in your own files—not in the employee's personnel file. Don't worry about the quality of your writing or the beauty of your presentation. You can even write entries by hand if you like.

Despite the informal nature of the log, however, there may come a time when other people will see it. If the employee sues your company, the performance log will be an important piece of evidence that the employee's lawyer will inspect. For this reason, while you need not worry about your writing style, you do need to be mindful of the content you include. Do not put anything in the log that you would not want to be read aloud in a public courtroom.

Here are some guidelines to follow when writing log entries:
- Include concrete and specific details—dates, times, places, names, numbers, and so on.
- Be accurate and don't exaggerate.
- Don't use slurs or other inappropriate or derogatory terms.
- Don't use language that could be construed as discriminatory or biased. Don't mention an employee's race, national origin, age, disability, gender, or sexual orientation when commenting on his or her performance. (See Chapter 2 for more about discriminatory language.)
- Avoid commenting on an employee's personality. Instead, concentrate on behavior, performance, conduct, and productivity.
- Stick to job-related incidents. Don't include entries about the employee's personal life or aspects of the employee that have nothing to do with the job.

If you talk to the employee informally about the conduct, or you decide to give an employee a written kudos or tickler or take disciplinary action, note this in your log as well, with a cross-reference to other documents by date.

Look at the sample performance log, below. Each entry is short and concise, requiring no more than two minutes to write. Where the manager provided a kudos or tickler, the manager did not go into details in the log, but rather referred to the other document itself. When the manager sits down to conduct the employee's formal evaluation, the manager can review this log along with the kudos and ticklers provided to the employee.

Follow your company's disciplinary process. Oral reminders and written warnings—two items mentioned in the sample performance log—are part of a disciplinary system. Your company may use different disciplinary documents and/or procedures. If so, of course, you should follow your company's policy.

Performance Log. At the end of this chapter, you'll find a blank performance log, which you can use to track noteworthy performance issues through the year. You'll also find a copy of the log in Appendix B and on the CD-ROM at the back of this book.

Sample Performance Log
CONFIDENTIAL

Employee Name: Paul Nolo

Employee Title: Copy editor

Date	Incident	Kudos/ Tickler/ Oral Reminder/ Written Warning (see personnel file)
1/2/20xx	Paul arrived 15 minutes late for work—did not call me to tell me that he would be late. Said he overslept.	N/A
2/3/20xx	Paul worked hard to ensure that he met the deadline for the Single Mothers series.	Kudos
3/1/20xx	Paul was 45 minutes late for his shift.	Informal oral reminder
4/4/20xx	Eleanor Lathom (reporter who worked with Paul on the Single Mother series) told me that she thought Paul was really easy to work with and helped her improve her writing.	Kudos
6/2/20xx	Paul had trouble editing a story on a jury verdict in an Alameda County Superior Court. Paul should have the knowledge to do this and should have been able to do it more quickly and on his own.	Tickler

Checklist: Documenting Performance. Use the following checklist to make sure that your performance log entries and other performance documentation is appropriate and effective. You'll also find a copy of the checklist in Appendix B and on the CD-ROM at the back of this book.

Checklist: Documenting Performance

When you write a performance log entry, kudos, or a tickler, or send an email about performance, make sure it meets these criteria:

- ☐ It contains concrete and specific details—dates, times, places, names, numbers, and so on.

- ☐ It is accurate and doesn't exaggerate.

- ☐ It doesn't contain slurs or other inappropriate or derogatory terms.

- ☐ It doesn't contain language that could be construed as discriminatory or biased.

- ☐ It doesn't focus on personality issues.

- ☐ It focuses on behavior, performance, conduct, and productivity.

- ☐ It is complete.

- ☐ It contains job-related incidents only. It doesn't include entries about the employee's personal life or aspects of the employee that have nothing to do with the job.

Documenting Ongoing Feedback

In addition to keeping a running performance log, you should give employees written feedback on their performance as it happens. Whenever an employee does something of note—either good or bad—don't wait until an appraisal meeting or written performance evaluation to let him or her know about it. Note it in your performance log and write a feedback memo for your employee. An effective performance evaluation system requires ongoing feedback.

This section provides two ways to document feedback for employees: kudos to compliment employees who are doing well and ticklers to alert employees who are struggling. You can call these types of notes anything you like, as long as you use them or something like them.

While kudos and ticklers are written forms of communication, don't forget the importance of oral communication as well. Don't just drop these in the employee's mailbox; instead, hand them to employees personally and offer to discuss them. When providing a tickler, explain that it is not a reprimand or discipline, but just a reminder to help keep the employee's performance on track.

Give Kudos When Employees Do Well

When you can praise an employee for a job well done, you should do so. Positive feedback not only improves employee morale, but also motivates employees to do better and improves your overall relationship with your team. People are more likely to accept and act on criticism when it's given in the context of a fair and positive employment relationship.

When employees do something especially good, give them kudos to commend them in writing or in an email. Kudos do not have to be elaborate—they are simply short notes that let employees know you notice and appreciate their efforts. Unlike the performance log, which is a tool for your reference, kudos are documents that you actually give to employees, placing copies in their personnel files. (Even if you send an email rather than handing the employee a piece of paper, you should put a copy of the email in the employee's personnel file.) Kudos can be informal; just observe the rules provided above for how to write performance log entries.

Reserve kudos for noteworthy occasions, such as unusually hard work or particularly successful efforts. Do not provide kudos when employees do the job you hired them to do—their paycheck is their reward for this. If you give kudos for everything an employee does satisfactorily, you will weaken the usefulness of kudos as a performance evaluation tool.

⚠ **Never make promises in kudos.** When writing kudos, do not say anything that the employee could interpret as a promise of continued employment or a promotion, such as "You have bright future at this company" or "You're going to go far here." If you do, a court might hold you to the promise. Simply thank the employee for doing well and leave it at that. (See Chapter 2 for more on this topic.)

💿 **Kudos.** At the end of this chapter, you'll find a blank kudos form, which you can use to give an employee positive feedback for good performance. You'll also find a copy of the form in Appendix B and on the CD-ROM at the back of this book.

Give Ticklers When Employees Veer Off Track

If an employee's performance begins to slip, do not wait until a formal evaluation meeting to let the employee know that you've noticed and are concerned. Write a tickler (or send an email) to let the employee know that he or she needs to make an adjustment.

Use a tickler to coach and counsel an employee, not to criticize or inspire fear. If you want, you can provide constructive advice or feedback in the tickler. Or you can simply remind an employee of a requirement or goal that you've set and note your concern that the employee won't meet it unless he or she performs differently. But don't overdo it: Ticklers are meant to be friendly tips or reminders from a caring boss, not a constant barrage of criticism from a manager who is watching the employee like a hawk.

Ticklers are not the same as written reprimands, which you use for more-serious performance and disciplinary problems. If the employee has done something seriously wrong, do not provide a tickler. Instead, discipline the employee appropriately.

Don't make ticklers long or elaborate. Don't spend a lot of time writing them, but do observe the same rules as those provided for how to write performance log entries. Give them to the employee, with a copy placed in the personnel file. (If you use email, place a copy of the email in the employee's personnel file.)

💿 **Tickler.** At the end of this chapter, you'll find a blank tickler form, which you can use to let employees know that their performance has fallen short of your expectations. You'll also find a copy of the form in Appendix B and on the CD-ROM at the back of this book.

Sample Kudos

Kudos to You

To: Paul Nolo

From: Amy Means

Cc:

Date: 2/3/20xx

Thanks for working so hard to meet the deadline for getting the Single Mothers series to production. I know that the stories were longer than we thought they would be, so they required more editing time than we had anticipated.

One of your goals for this year is to help decrease the number of deadlines the editorial department misses. Your work on this project was a step on the path to achieving that goal.

The fact that you made this deadline means that workers in production will not have to work overtime to get the series into the paper. I want you to know that I really appreciate your extra efforts.

We are only as good as our employees. Thanks for your efforts!

Sample Tickler

Tickler For You

To:	Paul Nolo
From:	Amy Means
Cc:	
Date:	6/2/20xx

This afternoon, you edited a story by Joey James on a jury verdict in the McClandish case. You had some trouble editing the story because you lack knowledge of the court system. For example, you inserted an error in Joey's story by saying that jury verdicts have to be unanimous. (FYI: A jury needs only a simple majority to reach a verdict in a civil case.)

You also had to take time to call Joey so that you could add a sentence explaining what a superior court is. This is something you should have been able to write on your own.

One of your personal goals for this year is to educate yourself on the court system so that you can edit legal stories more quickly and effectively. As you know, your next performance review is in October, so you have only four more months to achieve this goal.

I know you can get back on track!

Test Your Knowledge

Questions

1. A performance log is an informal document; you can even hand write it if you like. ☐ True ☐ False

2. Because the performance log resides in you own personal files, not the employee's personnel file, it can never be used against you in an employment lawsuit. ☐ True ☐ False

3. You should write a performance log entry for every day that an employee shows up to work. ☐ True ☐ False

4. When writing entries in a performance log, it's okay to leave the details to other documents, such as ticklers and kudos. ☐ True ☐ False

5. When documenting poor employee performance, document only the problematic results, not possible reasons for the performance problems. ☐ True ☐ False

6. It is not okay to use email as a way to give employees kudos and ticklers. ☐ True ☐ False

7. Only use kudos for noteworthy events; otherwise, you will dilute their effect. ☐ True ☐ False

8. A tickler and a written reprimand serve essentially the same function. ☐ True ☐ False

9. The best time to give feedback is in the formal setting of the year-end evaluation meeting. ☐ True ☐ False

10. Because ticklers might someday support a difficult management decision such as discipline or termination, they should be written in a very formal way. ☐ True ☐ False

Answers

1. **True.** A performance log is a personal tool for you to use. There is no need for you to spend time creating a formal document.

2. **False.** If an employee decides to sue your company, your performance log could become a piece of evidence. For this reason, don't write anything in the log that you wouldn't want a judge or jury to read.

3. **False.** Reserve log entries for noteworthy events.

4. **True.** As long as the details of the incident are recorded somewhere—such as in written kudos or a tickler—it's okay to leave the details out of your log. Be sure to note in your log, however, where those details reside by referring to the other document clearly.

5. **False.** If you know what contributed to an employee's poor performance—whether particular issues with the employee or problems outside of the employee's control (such as other departments' errors or delays)—document those reasons as well. Understanding why poor performance happens is the first step to correcting it.

6. **False.** Email is fine, as long as you follow the guidelines presented in this chapter and place a copy of the email in the employee's personnel file.

7. **True.** If you give kudos for everything an employee does adequately, kudos will lose their meaning.

8. **False.** A tickler is simply a reminder to help the employee get back on track. A written reprimand is far more severe and is a form of discipline.

9. **False.** Employees will be able to use your feedback to improve their performance only if they get it on an ongoing basis, throughout the year.

10. **False.** Ticklers are friendly concerns or reminders. They can be short and informal but should not contain anything that you wouldn't want a judge or jury to read.

Performance Log
CONFIDENTIAL

Employee Name: _____

Employee Title: _____

Date	Incident	Kudos/ Tickler/ Oral Reminder/ Written Warning (see personnel file)

Kudos to You

To: _____

From: _____

Cc: _____

Date: _____

_____

_____

_____

_____

_____

_____

_____

_____

_____

_____

_____

_____

_____

_____

_____

_____

_____

_____

_____

_____

_____

_____

We are only as good as our employees. Thanks for your efforts!

Tickler for You

To: _____

From: _____

Cc: _____

Date: _____

_____

_____

_____

_____

_____

_____

_____

_____

_____

_____

_____

_____

_____

_____

_____

_____

_____

_____

_____

_____

_____

_____

_____

I know you can get back on track!

Chapter 5

The Interim Meeting

Chapter Highlights

- At some point about halfway through the appraisal period, meet with the employee to discuss his or her progress toward meeting the requirements and goals you set for the year.

- At this meeting, review the employee's performance plan to make sure it still makes sense. If something needs to be changed, this is the time to do so.

- The interim meeting is not as in-depth or weighty as the year-end evaluation; it's simply time you set aside to check in with the employee.

- Do not write a formal evaluation for the interim meeting. Instead, write a memo after the meeting that documents what you and the employee discussed and decided.

After your employees have had some time to work toward their requirements and goals for the appraisal period, it's helpful to check in. To do this, schedule an interim performance meeting with each employee to discuss the employee's progress and make any needed adjustments to the performance plan. The interim meeting is not as in-depth as the year-end evaluation (discussed in Chapter 6), but rather a time you set aside to follow up with an employee on what has happened in the year so far and what adjustments need to made going forward for the rest of the appraisal period.

An interim meeting does not replace ongoing feedback. Previous chapters discuss the importance of providing your employees with ongoing, day-to-day feedback and coaching. Such feedback and coaching usually occur in the midst of other business—while discussing a project, in a few words before a meeting, over a celebratory lunch, and so on. The interim meeting does not take the place of providing ongoing feedback and coaching to an employee during the course of his or her work. Rather, it is a time you set aside to focus more fully on the employee's performance—time that isn't primarily about something else.

This chapter provides a brief overview of the interim meeting and how to prepare for and conduct it. Chapter 6 provides a more extensive discussion of the year-end evaluation meeting, and much of that discussion applies to the interim meeting as well. Because of this overlap, it's a good idea to read Chapter 6 (specifically the sections on writing the evaluation and conducting the evaluation meeting) in conjunction with this chapter when preparing for the interim meeting.

Scheduling the Meeting

For most jobs at most companies, the performance appraisal period is one year long. A good time to conduct an interim performance meeting, then, is about halfway through the appraisal period, or six months after the employee's last formal evaluation. In the case of a new employee, you would usually schedule this meeting six months after the employee started working for you and then conduct a formal, year-end performance evaluation six months after that (one year after the employee started the job).

Check in as often as possible. The model appraisal system described in this book suggests one interim meeting as a bare minimum. Ideally, you should review each employee's requirements and goals and his or her progress more frequently—perhaps every quarter or even every month. The more often you can check in with an employee, the better. This ensures that feedback and coaching happen regularly, and it keeps employees and their requirements and goals aligned with current business conditions. It also helps ensure that there won't be any surprises when the year-end appraisal rolls around.

For some jobs, especially those that are project-driven, it may be better to schedule the interim meeting at the halfway point or the end of a project, regardless of how much time has passed. Do whatever makes sense for the work the employee is doing. If that means you schedule the interim meeting only four months after setting the performance plan, so be it.

In all but the most extraordinary of circumstances, these interim meetings should be held in person. But if the employee works off site or overseas, you may not be able to schedule an in-person meeting. In such a situation, don't let geography stand in the way; hold the meeting over the phone. If you can find time in your schedule and room in your budget, however, it's much better to visit these employees where they work and hold the meeting there.

Preparing for the Meeting

When preparing for the interim meeting, remember that it does not involve an extensive review of the employee's work, nor does it require a formal written evaluation. Rather, it's an opportunity for the employee and you to take a step back and look at what is going on with the employee's work, solve any problems that have arisen, make sure the employee's performance plan is still appropriate, and assess whether the employee is on track to meet the job goals and requirements.

To prepare for the interim meeting, review the job description for the employee's position, along with the requirements and goals that you and the employee set at the beginning of the appraisal period. Then, review any work product or documentation that might show the employee's progress toward reaching those requirements and goals. Look at the records you've been keeping—a performance log, kudos, and ticklers—and anything else you think is important. You don't have to do the more exhaustive document review and information gathering described in Chapter 6 for the year-end evaluation, but do review everything that is readily available to you. Be prepared to give the employee specific advice and feedback about performance and progress—not merely vague impressions.

Both the employee and you will get more out of the interim meeting if the employee prepares for it, too. Give the employee a few days' notice and explain what you want to discuss. Ask the employee to spend some time thinking about how the past six months on the job have been—what's been good and what could be changed or improved. Other questions you should both ask yourselves include:

- Are these requirements and goals still important?
- Are they still realistic?
- Is the employee on track to meet them?
- If not, why not?
- What can be done to help?
- Are factors beyond the employee's control impeding the employee's performance? (These factors might include poor equipment, lack of resources, or an unusually difficult sales territory.)

In the case of employees who work overseas or off site, a self evaluation is particularly important, for the employee knows a lot more than you do about the context in which the employee is working.

Once you and the employee have spent a little time preparing, you are ready to meet.

Conducting the Meeting

Begin your meeting by giving the employee your overall impressions of his or her performance over the past six months (or however long it has been since you checked in). Note what the employee has done well and what he or she has done poorly. Share any compliments or complaints you've received from coworkers, customers, and so on.

When in doubt, say it. If there is a performance issue bubbling up, but you aren't sure whether to raise it now or wait until later, go ahead and mention it. Otherwise, you risk losing time that the employee could have had to correct the problem or, better yet, prevent it all together. Plus, you risk surprising the employee at the year-end evaluation, and surprises are never a good thing in the workplace.

Next, review the requirements and goals that the employee and you chose for the year. If they still seem realistic to you, discuss whether the employee is on track to meet them. If not, discuss why not and what can be done about it. If, after six months of working toward the requirements and goals, they now seem unrealistic or inappropriate, discuss how you can modify them.

Be sure to give the employee an opportunity to present his or her thoughts. What does the employee think he or she has accomplished over the past six months? Does the employee need any help to perform better? Does the employee need assistance or advice from you? Does the employee need additional or different resources from the department or the company? Has the employee encountered any obstacles that make it difficult to perform the job?

Wherever possible, be positive and encouraging. Motivate the employee. Send the message that the employee is important, that the employee's job is important, and that you respect and believe in the employee. Cheer on the employee and provide any encouragement that the employee might need to get past this point to the end of the year.

Where there have been problems, however, be honest and clear. Only through identifying the problems and searching for solutions can you get the employee back on track for his or her performance plan. And, if the employee has done anything that might lead to disciplinary action, you should discuss it now.

Your demeanor and attitude will make the difference between a meeting that is productive and one that is not. Always treat the employee with understanding and respect. Resist any temptation to become angry or emotional, and never engage in personal attacks (for example, don't tell an employee that he or she is "stupid" or "lazy").

After the Meeting

While the details of the conversation are still fresh in your mind, write a brief memo to the employee's personnel file that summarizes what you and the employee said. Include your views on the employee's performance at this interim point and describe what plans, if any, the two of you agreed on for the rest of the appraisal period.

The purpose of this memo is to document the meeting—both to aid your memory when the time comes to do the year-end appraisal and to use as evidence should the employee ever file a lawsuit (evidence of the employee's performance problems and awareness of the problems, as well as evidence of your good faith efforts to help the employee). Because this memo isn't a developmental tool, there is no reason to show it to the employee. It belongs in the employee's personnel file.

Test Your Knowledge

Questions

1. The interim meeting must take place six months into the appraisal period. ☐ True ☐ False

2. New employees don't need interim meetings. ☐ True ☐ False

3. If you hold an interim meeting, then there is no need to bother with ongoing coaching and feedback. ☐ True ☐ False

4. The interim meeting does not include a written evaluation. ☐ True ☐ False

5. The only purpose of the interim meeting is to get the employee on track toward meeting the performance plan that the two of you set at the beginning of the appraisal period. ☐ True ☐ False

Answers

1. **False.** It's generally a good idea to hold the interim meeting midway through the appraisal period, but a different timeframe might make more sense in some cases. Choose whatever makes sense for your workplace and the work that the employee is doing.

2. **False.** You should schedule interim meetings for all of your employees, regardless of how new they are. After all, you have the same expectations of new employees as you do of everyone else: to meet the requirements and goals that you have set. As a result, you need to go through the same steps with them to help them perform.

3. **False.** The interim meeting is meant to supplement, not replace, the ongoing coaching and feedback that you should be giving an employee throughout the appraisal period.

4. **True.** Although you should gather documents and collect your thoughts, you don't have to write a formal evaluation. You should, however, write up a memo summarizing what was said and agreed to during the meeting.

5. **False.** Although it's true that the interim meeting is a time to check in with the employee on his or her progress toward the requirements and goals, the interim meeting is also a time to review whether the requirements and goals are appropriate and realistic. In addition, the interim meeting is a perfect opportunity to cheer your employees on and give them the encouragement they need to make it through to the end of the appraisal period.

■

Chapter 6

The Year-End Performance Appraisal

Chapter Highlights

- For each employee, conduct a year-end appraisal, which consists of a formal written performance evaluation from you, a self-evaluation from the employee, and a meeting between you and the employee to review the evaluations and discuss requirements and goals for the coming year.

- When gathering information for the year-end evaluation, include objective data; records of significant incidents; notes of your own observations; and interviews with coworkers, customers, and other relevant people.

- When drawing conclusions about employee performance, determine whether the employee met the requirements and goals you set out at the beginning of the year, and figure out why or why not.

- When writing the evaluation, use concrete, specific details and a tone that is respectful toward the employee.

- Watch out for common errors when writing your evaluation, such as judging employees who are similar to you more favorably and giving undue weight to recent events that are fresh in your mind.

- Plan and prepare for your evaluation meeting. Choose a time when you won't be interrupted and a place that is private and conducive to working side by side (for example, a conference room). Create an agenda. Plan what you are going to say. Give the employee instructions on doing a self-evaluation—including, perhaps, a list of questions for the employee to answer and a description of documents that the employee should review.

- How you conduct yourself in the appraisal meeting is just as important as what you say. Be respectful, and plan for the employee's emotional response.

- Criticism alone will not improve performance. Don't just tell the employee that his or her performance was poor. Work with the employee to identify what went wrong and to develop a strategy for improvement. Also, don't forget to give praise when appropriate.

- As the last phase of the performance evaluation process, reassess job requirements and set personal goals for the coming year with the employee.

The performance appraisal process culminates at the end of the appraisal period—usually one year. At this time, you write a formal written performance evaluation, the employee does a self-evaluation, and you and the employee meet to discuss the evaluations and to look forward to the next year by reviewing job requirements and establishing new goals. All of these events together are called the year-end appraisal process.

As you now know, performance appraisal involves much more than this year-end appraisal process: It requires ongoing documentation and feedback—both of which will help make this year-end appraisal process go quickly and smoothly. Nonetheless, the year-end appraisal process is the most visible and formal part of the entire appraisal process. And it is the part that will get the most scrutiny if an employee files a lawsuit.

Your company's year-end appraisal process may differ from the process outlined here. For example, the written form your company uses may look nothing like the form this chapter provides, and your company may give you specific direction about what to cover during the meeting. Nonetheless, the legal and practical guidelines you will read here are good practices to follow when conducting your year-end appraisal process, no matter what form you use or which topics you cover.

Writing the Evaluation

Writing an effective year-end performance evaluation involves much more than simply completing blanks on a form; it involves gathering information, drawing conclusions, and summarizing your conclusions and supporting evidence in a written document. You must make the evaluation clear and useful to the employee and anyone else who might read it—including your human resources department and your company's lawyers, should it come to that. This section guides you through each step of writing a year-end evaluation.

Writing the Appraisal

1 Gather information

- Gather objective information (for example, sales numbers, call reports, productivity reports, and budgets).
- Gather qualitative information (for example, kudos, ticklers, performance logs, customer complaints, disciplinary memos, disciplinary actions, and samples of employee's work product).

2 Draw conclusions

- Assess performance: Did the employee meet the requirements and goals that you set for the year, and why or why not?
- Make sure you have avoided common appraisal errors.

3 Write the appraisal document

- Summarize conclusions.
- Provide best supporting evidence.

Canned Phrases Are No Good

If you find writing performance evaluations overwhelming, you are not alone. There is something about having to put pen to paper (or fingers to keyboard) to memorialize one's thoughts about an employee that fills managers with dread. Perhaps it is because writing an evaluation combines two things that make people uncomfortable: writing and criticizing.

Some managers cope with this discomfort by buying books filled with canned, prewritten phrases that they can copy into their reviews. Although these may simplify your life, they will not improve your employees' performance—which is, after all, your ultimate goal. Employees don't need artfully drafted prose; they need specifics. They need input. And they need your respect, consideration, and time. They get none of those things from canned phrases.

Moreover, if you use canned phrases that are obviously boilerplate, vague, or inapplicable to an employee's situation—particularly when criticizing an employee—it could get you into legal hot water if the employee later sues. A lawyer for the employee could discredit your evaluation by establishing that you copied phrases from a book rather than writing your own observations and conclusions.

The good news is that you don't need those canned phrases, anyway. If you follow the process described in this chapter—gather information, draw conclusions, and then write the evaluation—and don't worry too much about the quality of your writing, you'll do just fine. If, after reading this chapter, you still feel that your writing skills aren't good enough, consider making it one of your own performance goals for the coming year to take a short one-day seminar on writing.

Step One: Gathering Information

Although you may think you know in your gut how an employee has performed throughout the year, you cannot draw any firm conclusions until you've gathered and reviewed documents, reports, and other concrete evidence that reflect the employee's performance.

Objective Information

An easy way to begin is by gathering objective data that demonstrates the employee's performance and productivity. Objective data means facts that are not influenced by opinions. For example, a report showing that a call center answers an average of 100 calls per day is objective. If you wrote a report stating that the center did a "good job" of answering calls, however, that would be subjective—rather than objective—because it expresses your opinion about the facts. Objective data often comes in the form of numbers, and you can find it in all kinds of reports and documents that companies generate regularly, from budgets to shareholder disclosures. The following are examples of objective data:

- sales numbers
- earnings reports
- call records
- productivity reports
- deadline reports
- output and production records
- budget reports, and
- time records.

Objective data is useful because it is unassailable by the employee or by anyone else (such as a judge or jury) who might question the basis for your evaluation, especially if it is critical. Objective facts are not based on opinions or judgments and cannot be influenced by illegal considerations such as a person's race or age. (Chapter 2 discusses factors that are illegal to consider.)

Qualitative Information

As useful as objective data is, however, it alone will not give you the complete picture of the employee's performance for the year.

For one thing, there may be factors to consider behind, or in addition to, the objective data. For example, say one job requirement for newspaper editors is to edit at least seven articles per night, and you have an editor who edits an average of eight articles a night during the appraisal period. That objective fact indicates that the editor is productive. The editor may be able to edit so quickly, however, by not being thorough and by allowing numerous errors to slip through. A manager who did not look behind the objective deadline report would miss the editor's carelessness and inaccuracy. Thus, subjective, qualitative (as opposed to objective, quantitative) information may be necessary to give you the whole picture.

Qualitative data is also important because you may not be able to measure some information about an employee's performance objectively—or at all. For example, if you manage a salesperson, you might want to know if customers trust the employee. Although sales numbers might provide indirect evidence, more compelling would be interviews with customers and a review of any complaints or compliments.

To gather information not reflected in the objective data, look for records of significant incidents that demonstrate the employee's performance—both positive and negative. If you gave any kudos or ticklers to the employee throughout the year (as suggested in Chapter 4), you will already have a record of incidents that you can use. Customer and vendor complaints and compliments are also records of significant incidents, as are any documents of disciplinary action against the employee.

Also, talk to people who work with the employee: clients or customers, coworkers, other managers or supervisors, human resources personnel, vendors, and so on. Solicit specific feedback from those who have worked with the employee, asking about any particular events or projects that reflect upon the employee's performance. Check with other managers and your human resources department to see if they have additional records on the employee.

Review records—such as a performance log—of your own observations. If you are in the habit of saving email or phone messages, look through these to see if you have any that relate to a noteworthy event or an example of the employee's performance.

If it is feasible, look at a sampling of the employee's work product.

Finally, look at a copy of the employee's performance appraisal from the previous year and the employee's job description.

When the Employee Works in a Different Country

Gathering information about employees on overseas assignments is challenging. Any information you collect will be from a context and culture that is different from the one you work in at home, and you may not fully understand all of the factors at play. This context involves unique societal, physical, and economic challenges. (For example, poor sales figures may really be the result of a fluctuating monetary exchange rate.) Sometimes, what looks like odd, inexplicable behavior is really the employee adapting to his or her situation. There may be cultural constraints on the employee performing well.

Some multinational companies have different forms and processes for assessing employees who are on foreign assignments; others do not. If you are in a company that uses the same forms and standards for all employees, regardless of context, then you must somehow make your standardized form work for international employees. You may not have had a chance to adequately observe the employee, to assess the context in which the employee works, or to gather the necessary information.

What to do? Be aware of the issue and talk to the employee about it. Make sure that the employee addresses the issue in his or her self-appraisal. Use appraisals from coworkers and others who do understand the context. And, of course, ask for help from your human resources department.

Step Two: Drawing Conclusions

Review the evidence you have gathered. You must determine whether the employee met the requirements and goals that you set for the year and why or why not. The "why" is perhaps the most important part of the process, because it will tell you whether the responsibility for any shortcomings—or any successes—should fall on the employee. And, if the employee failed to meet a requirement or goal, it will help you develop strategies for improvement.

Checklist: Information to Gather for a Performance Appraisal. Use the following checklist to make sure that you've left no stone unturned in collecting information to consider when writing your performance appraisal. You'll also find a copy of the checklist in Appendix B and on the CD-ROM at the back of this book.

☑ Checklist:
Information to Gather for a Performance Appraisal

As you prepare to write your performance appraisal, gather the following documents and records.

Objective Data:

☐ sales numbers

☐ earnings reports

☐ call records

☐ productivity reports

☐ deadline reports

☐ output and production records

☐ budget reports

☐ attendance records

☐ training or continuing education records

☐ time records

Critical Incidents:

☐ kudos

☐ ticklers

☐ customer complaints or compliments

☐ disciplinary notices

☐ personnel file

Personal Observations:

☐ performance log

☐ notes, emails, and/or phone messages

Third-Party Interviews:

☐ other managers

☐ clients/customers

☐ coworkers

☐ vendors

Other:

☐ work product

☐ current job description

☐ previous year's performance appraisal, including requirements and goals for the current year

Assessing Performance

If you're feeling overwhelmed by the information you've accumulated or unsure of how to synthesize it, start by looking at the employee's requirements and goals for the appraisal period. For each, look at all the items you have that relate to it. You might even try making lists—or literally separating the papers into stacks on a table or the floor—to help you organize what you've got. Then, for each requirement and goal, ask yourself the following questions:

• Has the employee met this requirement or goal?
• Why or why not?
• How do I know this?
• What is the supporting evidence?
• What was the impact on the department? On the company?
• How can the employee do better?
• How can I do a better job of supporting the employee?
• How can the company do a better job of supporting the employee?

When faced with a performance or productivity problem, look beyond the employee's willingness (or lack thereof) to perform or make an effort. Consider other factors that may have played a role, such as the work environment, coworkers, other departments, or issues outside of work that could have affected the employee's performance. For example, simply telling the employee to work harder or do better will accomplish little if the employee's supervisor is the true cause of the problem. Similarly, if the employee doesn't have the necessary skills to do the job or is having health or familial problems outside of the office, you'll have to take these factors into account when shaping a solution. (See "When Things Get Personal," below, for more on this issue.)

When Things Get Personal

It would be nice if employees could leave their personal problems at home, but they can't. A tough personal life can derail even the most conscientious employee.

For a manager, this is a particularly difficult issue: Your employee is not obligated to tell you about personal, nonwork difficulties, and even if you know about the situation, you're usually in no position to dictate solutions. The most you can do is offer understanding and flexibility—which is often just what the employee wants and needs. Consider the following:

> **EXAMPLE:** Ever since Rose's teenage son was arrested for drug use, Rose has been useless at work after 3:00 p.m. She worries about what he's doing every day after school. She spends afternoons fretting and distracted until she leaves at 5:00 p.m. Her productivity has dropped off significantly. Rose's boss, Jose, doesn't want to lose Rose, who is a good worker, but he also can't afford to have her wasting her afternoons in this way. Jose suggests a flexible work schedule to Rose. Rather than working 9:00 a.m. to 5:00 p.m., she can work from 7:00 a.m. to 3:00 p.m. That way, her work schedule will coincide with her son's schedule and she can be home when he gets out of school. Rose accepts the new schedule and her productivity returns to its old level.

If all else fails, resort to your discipline system. No matter how sympathetic you are to an employee's situation, you can't allow an intractable personal problem to infect your workplace.

Note, however, that if the personal problem involves a medical condition, a possible disability claim, or a need for family and medical leave, the practical problem of a poorly performing employee has just become a legal issue for your company and you. Do not try to deal with the situation on your own. Alert your human resources department or legal counsel immediately.

If an employee is new to the job, consider the following issues before reaching a conclusion about the employee's performance:

- Did you give the employee adequate training? For example, if the job requires using an accounting system, did you teach the employee how to use it? If not, and if the employee is taking too long to complete assignments, the employee may be struggling with a system he or she doesn't understand.

- Does the employee have the skills necessary for the job? For example, if you hired a talented new artist who doesn't know how to use computer graphics programs, he or she won't be able to design computer graphics for you.

- Does the employee understand what you expect? For instance, if you hired a retail salesperson, he or she may not know that you expect your salespeople to clean the store when business is slow.

- Have you provided the employee with adequate tools and resources for doing the job? For example, if you give only one computer and printer to three employees to share, this lack of equipment might delay work—a delay that won't be their fault.

- Does your company have rules or systems that make it difficult for the employee to do the job? For instance, if you allow a supplier to deliver raw materials to you at the last minute, you make it difficult for your employees to produce what's expected in time.

If the employee has been in the job for a while, think about the following possible causes for the drop in performance:

- Has something changed in the employee's work situation that might explain the trouble? For example, does the employee have a new supervisor, new coworkers, or new customers who are difficult to work with? Or does the employee have new duties or responsibilities with which he or she might need help?

- Has anything happened in the employee's personal life that could be affecting his or her work, such as a new child, a family health problem, or a divorce? (See "When Things Get Personal," above, for guidance on dealing with this type of situation.)

- Has the employee developed a substance abuse problem or a mental health problem, such as depression or anxiety? If so, consult with your human resources department or with your company's attorney. Not only is this a time for tact and understanding on your part, it's a situation that might fall within the scope of the federal Americans With Disabilities Act and similar state laws.

> **Checklist: Assessing Performance.** Use the following checklist to help you evaluate how well an employee has performed and why. You'll also find a copy of the checklist in Appendix B and on the CD-ROM at the back of this book.

☑ Checklist: Assessing Performance

Consider the following questions when assessing performance:

- ☐ Has the employee met this requirement or goal?
- ☐ Why or why not?
- ☐ How do I know this?
- ☐ What is the supporting evidence?
- ☐ What was the impact on the department? On the company?
- ☐ How can the employee do better?
- ☐ How can I do a better job of supporting the employee?
- ☐ How can the company do a better job of supporting the employee?

Consider the following possible reasons for poor performance:

- ☐ Did I give the employee adequate training?
- ☐ Does the employee have the skills necessary for the job?
- ☐ Does the employee understand what I expect?
- ☐ Have I provided the employee with adequate tools and resources?
- ☐ Are there any rules or systems in place that make it difficult for the employee to perform well?
- ☐ Has anything changed in the employee's work situation?
- ☐ Has anything happened in the employee's personal life that could be affecting his or her work?
- ☐ Has the employee developed a substance abuse or mental health problem?

Common Appraisal Errors

As you review the information and draw conclusions about an employee's performance, be mindful of some common pitfalls that can lead you down the wrong path—and undermine the value of your appraisal. Succumbing to pitfalls can also damage your credibility in the eyes of your employees and leave your company vulnerable in lawsuits. Common pitfalls include:

- **Leniency error.** Studies show that the most common error managers make when evaluating performance is to rate employees too highly. This is called "leniency error," and if allowed to seep into your system, it will undercut everything you are trying to do. It will destroy your credibility (both with those you supervise and with those who supervise you); it will create the impression that positive reviews and pay raises are not linked to good performance; it will place your company in a precarious position should an employee sue; and it will make it more difficult to develop employee skills. After all, it you give mediocre or poor performers positive reviews, how can you expect them to do any work to improve? (For more information on leniency error, listen to the interview with Amy DelPo, included on the CD-ROM at the back of this book.)

- **The blame game.** Don't blame employees just because things are going poorly or take credit when things are going well. When looking at the "why" behind someone's performance, you might have to acknowledge that you were the source of the problem or, if something good happened, that you weren't behind it. Give credit where credit is due, and take responsibility when the fault lies with you. Your employees will recognize your honesty and respond accordingly.

- **Focusing on first impressions.** Don't allow your first impressions of an employee—whether good or bad—to color your opinions. It is only natural for people to judge others quickly, but, as a manager, you must be vigilant and not let this happen. It is unfair and unprofessional, and will create problems in your workforce. Good employees who can't seem to do anything right because they made a poor first impression will quickly learn that there is no use in trying. And bad employees to whom nothing negative sticks because you liked them right away will have no incentive to do well.

- **Liking those like you.** Don't judge more favorably employees who are similar to you and judge less favorably employees who are different from you. This is particularly troubling when—even unconsciously—you do so based on legally protected characteristics such as race, gender, nationality, sexual orientation, or religion. (See Chapter 2 for a discussion of legally protected characteristics.) But beyond these, be mindful not to judge your workers differently based on such things as your shared personality traits, values, skill sets, political opinions, hobbies, outlook, and the like.

- **The "halo/horns effect."** Don't allow one aspect of the employee's performance—whether good or bad—to blind you to everything else the employee does. Almost every employee has positive and negative work attributes. It's up to you as the manager to consider all aspects of an employee's performance.

- **Calling everyone "average."** Don't try to play it safe by judging all employees as average. You may think that no one will complain if everyone gets essentially the same review—but that is exactly the problem. If an employee performs exceptionally well but gets the same review as an employee who performs poorly, you've created a disincentive for the good employee to continue performing so well. And you've created an equally powerful disincentive for the bad employee to improve. If your evaluations should become evidence in a lawsuit, having judged everyone the same means your reviews aren't accurate and are therefore a big problem for your company in the courtroom.

- **Placing more weight on recent events.** Don't overemphasize an employee's recent performance. It might be fresh in your mind and, therefore, seem more important than things that happened in the past, but it's unfair and contrary to the goals of the review for you to fail to assess the employee's performance over the entire appraisal period.

- **Stereotyping employees.** As explained in Chapter 2, stereotypes based on characteristics protected by law (such as race, gender, nationality, religion, and so on) are illegal. But basing decisions on even legal stereotypes can damage the fairness and accuracy of your evaluation. Don't make assumptions; base your conclusions on objective and qualitative information.

- **Review based on fear.** Sometimes, managers will soften their reviews because they are afraid of making employees mad or hurting their feelings. Although you should always use tact and respect, downplaying poor performance only leads to trouble. Not only do you rob your department and your company of the benefits of the performance appraisal process, but also you risk sabotaging your ability to terminate the employee should the need arise. Manage with courage and write an honest, straightforward review.

Fortunately, the more information you have, the less likely you are to fall prey to one of these pitfalls. You can inoculate yourself further by following the observation and documentation process outlined in Chapter 4. Still, all managers are human, so it's useful to glance through a list of these common errors at the end of every evaluation to make sure that you haven't slipped.

Politics Can Get in the Way

Organizations are political entities, so it is not surprising that when managers conduct performance appraisals, they take into account the political consequences of what they say and write. According to an article in the February 2005 issue of the journal Group and Organizational Management, executives admit that accuracy is not always the goal when they conduct performance appraisals. Rather, the goal is survival—both for themselves and for the employee. If a manager rates an employee highly, it might be because the employee deserves it, or it might be for other reasons: to protect the employee from the consequences of a negative appraisal, cover up poor performance in the department, or preserve work relationships and avoid conflict, for example.

Checklist: Common Performance Appraisal Errors. Use the following checklist to help you make sure that you haven't fallen into a common appraisal trap. You'll also find a copy of the checklist in Appendix B and on the CD-ROM at the back of this book.

☑ Checklist:
Common Performance Appraisal Errors

After you have drawn conclusions about an employee's performance, ask yourself the following questions. If you can answer yes to any of them, then you've fallen prey to a common appraisal error—and you must rethink your conclusions.

☐ Have I rated the employee more highly than he or she deserves?

☐ Did I unfairly blame the employee for bad events or unfairly take credit (or give credit to someone else) for good events?

☐ Did I allow my first impressions to color what the employee did during this appraisal period?

☐ Did I allow one aspect of the employee's performance to dominate?

☐ Did I judge the employee more favorably because of our similarities?

☐ Did I judge the employee less favorably because of our differences?

☐ Did I gravitate to the middle to make this evaluation easier on myself?

☐ Did I ignore anything exceptionally good or bad about the employee's performance?

☐ Did I unfairly paint the employee as being either all good or all bad?

☐ Did I place too much weight on recent events?

☐ Have I made assumptions about or stereotyped the employee?

☐ Have I accurately described the employee's performance without fear of making the employee mad or of hurting the employee's feelings?

Step Three: Summarizing Your Conclusions and Evidence in a Document

After you have collected your observations and drawn conclusions about the employee's performance, it's time to document them, along with the supporting evidence. Most companies provide a performance evaluation form for this purpose, although some ask managers to write their review as a narrative. If your company provides a form, use it. If not, you can use the sample performance evaluation form provided at the end of this chapter or create your own.

The sample performance evaluation form contains a series of sections—one for each requirement or goal. Address the employee's job requirements first, in order of their importance, and then turn to the goals, again in order of priority. (You should have prioritized both when setting them with the employee, as explained in Chapter 3.) For each requirement or goal, the form provides a numbered area for you to do the following:

1. Give the priority level of the requirement or goal.
2. State the requirement or goal.
3. Write your conclusion as to whether the employee met the requirement or goal.
4. Give the reasons and evidence supporting your conclusions.
5. Record the employee's comments.
6. Jot down notes after your evaluation meeting with the employee.

There is also a place on the form for you to note any disciplinary problems that arose during the year.

For each requirement or goal, give your narrative evaluation of the employee's performance in areas 3 and 4 of the sample appraisal form at the end of the chapter: In area 3, state your conclusion as to how successfully the employee met the requirement or goal you are writing about; then, in area 4, explain the basis for your conclusion, using specific details and examples. You'll complete areas 5 and 6 at the appraisal meeting. If there are disciplinary issues to address, explain them at the end of the form.

When explaining the support for your conclusion, choose your best evidence. Although you may have a great deal of material, there's no point in overwhelming the employee with every example when a few key ones will do. Don't ignore or forget about those other examples, though; you'll need them if the employee ever files a lawsuit.

Follow these guidelines when writing the narrative portions of the evaluation:

- Use concrete and specific details—dates, times, places, names, and numbers. When you can, refer to specific documents that support your conclusions—for example, a tickler, kudos, an email, or a memo.
- Use the active, not passive, voice. Clearly identify who did (or did not do) what—for example, instead of "Research has been late," write "Mary turned in her research late twice."
- Move from the general to the specific: Start by summarizing your thoughts, then give specific examples or evidence.
- Use a tone that shows respect for the employee.
- Never use slurs, inappropriate or derogatory terms, or language that could be construed as discriminatory or illegally biased. (See Chapter 2 for more about discriminatory language.)
- Be accurate. Don't exaggerate or embellish.
- Provide more support for particularly high or low ratings.
- Make sure each entry is complete, so that anyone reading it can understand your conclusions and the basis for each.
- Be brief. Don't take ten sentences to say what can be said in one or two.

When you are done, read through the form to ensure that, as a whole, it reflects what you think about the employee. Do you believe all of the statements you made are true? Is the appraisal consistent with the feedback you gave the employee throughout the year? If not, then the review may come as a surprise to the employee, which means that you need to improve your ongoing feedback skills throughout the year and that you have a tough year-end appraisal meeting ahead of you.

The following is an example of how to complete the sample performance evaluation form included at the end of this chapter. It illustrates how to fill out the various sections for any given job requirement or goal.

Performance Evaluation Form. At the end of this chapter, you'll find a blank performance evaluation form. You'll also find a copy of the form in Appendix B and on the CD-ROM at the back of this book.

Sample Performance Evaluation

Performance Evaluation

Employee: _Paul Nolo_

Job Title: _Copy editor_

Appraiser: _Amy Means_

Job Title: _Copy desk chief_

Appraisal Period: 1/11/20xx through 1/11/20xx

Requirements (ranked in order from most important to least important):

1. Requirement priority number _1_

2. State the requirement: One requirement of Paul's job is to miss no more than one deadline per month.

3. Did the employee meet the requirement? Yes. As the attached Deadline Report shows, Paul missed an average of .078 deadlines per month during the appraisal period.

4. Explain: Paul did not meet this requirement last year, so we spent a significant amount of time at last year's appraisal meeting figuring out why—and what Paul could do to improve. Throughout this year, I personally observed Paul making a concerted effort to meet this requirement. He received no ticklers this year reminding him to talk less while at work (he received five last year), and he took fewer personal phone calls. As the attached time report shows, he reduced his editing average time per column inch from two minutes last year to one and a half minutes this year.

5. Employee's comments: _____

6. Appraisal meeting notes: _____

Presenting the Written Evaluation to the Employee

There is much debate among managers and human resources professionals about when to meet with the employee—before or after the manager writes the appraisal.

Some experts suggest that you meet with the employee before you write the evaluation. They argue that you don't really have all the information you need to write your evaluation until you have spoken to the employee and heard what he or she has to say.

This book, however, recommends that you write the appraisal first and then meet with the employee. The very act of writing the appraisal forces you to organize your thoughts and conclusions, which will make your meeting more meaningful than it would be if you relied on only your memory and impressions. On the sample evaluation form included at the end of this chapter, there is room for both employee comments and meeting notes. If you learn something during the meeting that truly alters your conclusions, you can revise the appraisal after the meeting.

Obviously, you must do what your company's system requires. But, if your company requires you to meet before you write, you should still complete the first two steps of the writing process—gathering information and drawing conclusions—before the meeting. That way, you will be prepared and the meeting will be useful.

Planning the Appraisal Meeting

Now that you have written your initial portions of the evaluation, it's time to plan and prepare to meet with the employee.

Choosing a Time and Place

Given the importance of the year-end performance appraisal meeting, be sure to set aside sufficient time—at least an hour. Nothing feels more insulting to an employee than to receive a performance appraisal from a manager who is distracted or in a rush. Consult with the employee to choose a day that will work for both of you and be relatively stress-free. Choose a time when phone calls and interruptions will be minimal.

Then, pick an appropriate place to meet. If you can, avoid your office, because it is your space, the base of your power, and it is unlikely that the employee will feel as comfortable there as in a more neutral environment. Find a private place where other people cannot see or hear you. A conference room is usually ideal, unless it has a lot of glass that allows people to look in. If you can, find a place with a big table so that you can spread out your records and documents and sit next to (rather than across from) the employee—a subtle but important affirmation that the evaluation is meant to be a discussion, not a lecture.

Preparing the Employee for the Self-Evaluation

After you schedule the meeting, give the employee an idea of what will happen at the meeting. Explain that you will be talking about the past year's performance and that you will be using a written evaluation as a framework for that discussion.

Virtually all effective performance evaluation systems—including the one presented in this book—ask employees to evaluate themselves as part of the process. Research has shown that having employees evaluate themselves puts them in a better frame of mind for evaluation meetings and makes them more satisfied with the process. Employees who evaluate themselves tend to be less defensive, and they tend to view both the appraiser (you) and the appraisal process as fair.

Despite these benefits, some managers dislike asking employees to do a self-evaluation. A manager may be concerned about what to do if an employee's self-evaluation does not match the manager's evaluation. If you share this concern, know that it is okay—even beneficial—for the evaluations to be different. Indeed, total agreement is not the goal; rather, the goal is for the employee and you to communicate.

In doing the self-evaluation, the employee should review much of the same materials as you: the job description, performance plan, requirements and goals, ticklers and kudos, reports, last year's evaluation, and so on. (You could even give the employee a copy of the "Information to Gather for a Performance Evaluation" checklist, above.)

Employees can either write the self-evaluation or simply come to the meeting prepared to discuss their own views on their performance. Some companies even have a form for employees to complete. In any event, the employee should prepare to answer the following questions:

- For each of the employee's requirements and goals, did the employee meet that requirement or goal, and how?
- What things has the employee done over the review period that he or she is most proud of?

- In what ways was the employee disappointed in his or her performance?
- Looking to next year, in what ways would the employee like to improve or change?
- Is there anything more that the company, the department, or the supervisor/manager can do to help support the employee's work or improve his or her performance?
- Is the employee unclear about any of his or her requirements, his or her goals, or what is expected of him or her in the current job?

After the meeting, you will finalize the evaluation. If the employee wrote a self-evaluation, attach it to your evaluation. If the employee did not write the self-evaluation, then you should incorporate information from the evaluation that the employee gave you at the meeting into your form.

Finally, tell the employee that, at the end of the meeting, the two of you will reassess the job requirements and set new performance goals for the coming year, so the employee should come prepared for that discussion as well.

Conducting the Appraisal Meeting

For most employees, the performance appraisal meeting is the most significant and important interaction that the employee has with the manager all year. Not only does the manager assess the employee's performance for the entire appraisal period, but the manager also gives advice, offers coaching on ways to improve, and sets new goals for the upcoming year.

This is also an important meeting for managers. This is your chance to get feedback from the employee to help you support the employee, improve your own performance as a manager, and improve the performance of your department. What does the employee think of the job? Of the workplace? Of your company as a whole? Has the employee encountered any obstacles within the workplace that make it difficult to do the job well? Does the employee see areas in which you or other managers could help employees improve their performance and productivity? Are there resources employees need that you aren't giving them? If the employee works overseas or off site, be sure to ask the employee to describe the context and culture in which he or she works—and how these issues may affect performance.

Meeting Atmosphere

When you meet with the employee, the feeling in the room should be business-like, yet friendly. Because this is a collaborative process between you and the employee, you want the employee to feel relaxed, comfortable, and safe, so set a congenial, relatively informal tone. Nonetheless, this is an important meeting, so you don't want to go so informal that you begin to show a lack of respect for the process. The meeting tone should feel like "business casual"—not as relaxed as blue jeans, but not as formal as a suit.

To set this sort of tone, be friendly when you greet the employee. Smile and thank the employee for coming. Spend the first few minutes on appropriate small talk: Ask about the employee's day or a recent vacation. If you and the employee always talk about a local sports team or each other's children, then engage in a little of that now.

Also, set the room up so that you sit beside each other at a table or in comfortable chairs, rather than across a desk from each other.

Small talk is nice, but don't fake it. If you and the employee never talk about anything but work, forced small talk is going to strike a false note. For example, if you have never discussed the employee's children before, don't suddenly become interested in how they are doing. Whatever you say to try to put the employee at ease, it should be appropriate and genuine.

Beware of jokes. Some managers might think that a few jokes are just the right way to set a friendly tone, but humor is a matter of personal taste: What might be funny to you may offend the employee or at least give the employee the impression that you aren't taking things seriously. Often the person telling the joke has no idea that it's going to offend until it's landed with a thud. To be on the safe side, avoid jokes altogether. There are other, less risky ways to be friendly.

When opening the discussion of the employee's performance, be conversational. Be warm, upbeat, and supportive: Focus on "we"—you and the employee—for example, "I'm excited that we have this opportunity to sit down and talk about your work and goals."

Meeting Agenda

Taking some time to explain the order of events at the meeting will make the whole process go more smoothly. Feel free to conduct the meeting in a way that feels natural and appropriate for your employee and you. Below is a suggested sequence of events and topics.

First, **start with some introductory remarks.** Thank the employee for coming. Explain why performance appraisal is important. Make it clear that you take this seriously and expect the employee to do so as well.

Second, if you didn't **give each other copies of your evaluations** before the meeting, do so now.

Third, **go through each requirement and goal.** The employee should give the self-evaluation first, and then you should give your opinion.

If you have judged the employee much more negatively than the employee has judged him or herself, consider why. Ask the employee for his or her thoughts. Consider them, and then give the employee insight into your own thought process. Keep an open mind: Could some of what the employee is saying be true? If, in the end, you stand by your initial conclusions, reassure the employee that you have considered everything that the employee has said, but that you haven't changed your mind. Explain why.

Be sure to give the employee enough time to talk. If you don't listen to your employee, you undermine the appraisal process. This is not a time for you to issue pronouncements. You don't want to miss this opportunity to learn about your company from someone who works on the front lines.

After you have evaluated the employee's past performance, move away from the appraisal portion of the meeting to **reassess the requirements** that apply to the employee's job. (See "Reassessing Job Requirements and Setting Goals," below, for more on this part of the conversation.)

Then it's time for you and the employee together to look forward and **choose goals for the coming year.** (See "Reassessing Job Requirements and Setting Goals," below, for more about this topic.)

Finally, **end the meeting on a positive note.** Thank the employee for the time and effort he or she took to prepare for and participate in the meeting, and leave the employee with words of encouragement for the coming year.

Checklist: Agenda for the Year-End Appraisal Meeting. This checklist will help you plan what to cover at your meeting, and in what order. You'll also find a copy of the checklist in Appendix B and on the CD-ROM at the back of this book.

✓ Checklist:
Agenda for the Year-End Appraisal Meeting

Although you should conduct the meeting in a way that feels natural and appropriate to you, here is a good sequence of events and topics to cover:

☐ Start with some introductory remarks.

☐ Give each other copies of your evaluation.

☐ Go through each requirement and goal.

☐ Reassess the job requirements.

☐ Choose goals for the coming year.

☐ End the meeting on a positive note.

Your Tone and Conduct

The words you use and the way you conduct yourself in the meeting are just as important—perhaps more so—than what you say. If your manner puts the employee off or makes the employee defensive, then the employee won't hear what you have to say, anyway. Pay attention to what some experts call "relationship management"—be sensitive to the feelings your words will create. You know the employee will have an emotional response to what you say, and you can usually predict what that response will be. It is foolish, then, not to take that response into consideration when conducting an evaluation meeting. Too often, managers ignore their employees' emotions. But ignoring them doesn't make them go away; it often makes them worse.

Think about the process from the employee's perspective. Evaluating employees may be routine for you. For the employee, however, it's a once-a-year opportunity to get your full focus and attention on the employee's job and career path. It is, therefore, a vital meeting for the employee. Don't make jokes, and don't treat it lightly. Even if the meeting feels like an annoying chore to you, don't let it show.

Instead, show respect for the meeting, the process, and, above all, the employee. This means really listening to what the employee has to say rather than simply waiting for the employee to finish talking so that you can launch into your evaluation. It also means showing the employee that you are listening—by taking notes, asking about key points, making comments, making eye contact, and nodding your head. When the employee says something important, say it back to the employee in your own words. If the employee has raised any concerns, address them squarely. Even though you are a superior to the employee, do not act superior. Consider yourself as an equal who wants to work with the employee to make the employee, the department, and the company succeed.

Do not use the meeting as a forum for attacking the employee. The purpose is to help the employee improve, not to belittle or punish the employee for past mistakes. Be empathetic toward the employee: Use the meeting to help the employee develop strategies for improving performance in the future.

When you have to criticize, remember that criticism alone is not helpful. You must combine it with a conversation about why the poor performance happened in the first place, the impact it had on the department and the company, and what can be done—by the employee, by you, and by the company—to improve. For strategies on how to deliver negative feedback effectively, see "Delivering Criticism," below.

Delivering Criticism

Most of us have heard this advice for polite conversation: "If you don't have anything nice to say, don't say anything at all." During a performance appraisal, however, you shouldn't follow this advice. Holding your tongue when an employee needs to hear negative feedback is not only counterproductive, it can also be dangerous should you end up in court. Your employees won't gain the benefit of your insight, and your company won't enjoy the legal protection that comes from documenting performance problems as they happen.

Instead of avoiding criticism, learn to criticize in a way that is constructive. If you give helpful criticism—that is, criticism that tells the employee how to improve—you're actually being a positive force for change. In other words, don't throw up your hands and tell the employee "everything is rotten; end of meeting." Instead, identify the problems and then reassure the employee that help—in the form of you—has arrived.

Here are some tips on how to give positive, constructive criticism:

- **Be straightforward.** If you are going to criticize an employee's performance, do so clearly and confidently. Be plainspoken and direct. Don't bury the criticism in qualifiers like "I think," "It seems to me that," or "You may disagree, but." This is insulting and counterproductive to an employee who wants to do his or her best.

- **Be specific.** You should never be vague when providing feedback, and this is especially true when the feedback is negative. Vague criticism can sound like an attack: "Your sales were terrible" is a lot more painful to hear than "Your sales were 10 percent below the target." Also, vagueness does not foster problem solving. The more specific you are, the easier it will be to develop a strategy for improvement. Tie your feedback to specific requirements and goals.

- **Be balanced.** Rarely does an employee do everything poorly. Look at the whole of the employee's performance. Identify what the employee has done well and what the employee has done poorly, and then deliver the news in a way that is proportional to the employee's performance. Don't get so involved in the problems that you ignore or downplay the good stuff.

- **Be helpful.** If an employee is performing poorly, it's not just the employee's problem, it's your problem, too. Telling employees that they are doing poorly and leaving it up to them to figure out how to do better is not only cruel, it is also waste of time. Give concrete suggestions on what they should do differently. Tell employees what to do and what not to do. If you don't know, then ask the employee what he or she thinks might help. If neither of you can figure it out, then it might be time to get outside assistance—from someone else in the company, maybe, or from a consultant.

- **Be encouraging.** Employees want to please their bosses and want to feel that their bosses have confidence in them. When you deliver criticism, part of what upsets employees is the feeling that they have disappointed you and that you don't think they are valuable. You must nip these feelings in the bud by reassuring employees that you still value them and believe they can do the job. Here, too, be specific. Explain why you value and believe in the employee.

Your review should not be a surprise to the employee. If it is, then you must be prepared for the employee to be defensive. Try not to let the defensiveness get to you—don't react to it. Rather, try to listen through it so that you hear what the employee has to say. Not only will you glean valuable information this way, you will also defuse the situation by hearing out the employee.

Finally, don't forget to say something positive when you can. Identify what you like about the employee's performance, and focus on it. Don't be vague—be specific and concrete. Don't make the employee feel cheated by giving compliments only as a set up for criticism—as in "Your coworkers really like you, but you spend too much time talking to them." Give a compliment and end it with a period.

Reassessing Job Requirements and Setting Goals

In the final portion of the year-end evaluation meeting, you and the employee review the requirements for the employee's position and choose new goals for the employee for the coming year.

Reassessing Job Requirements

As you may recall from Chapter 3, job requirements are related to the job, not the employee. Because of this, they generally stay the same from year to year. There are times, however, when the requirements will change. For example, if the company's strategic plan changes significantly, you may need to change the requirements for a particular job. Another common reason for changing job requirements is that technology either eliminates or changes the set of skills needed to perform a job.

Whether the job requirements should change or not, the year-end meeting is a good time to reassess. Together, you and the employee should review the requirements and talk about whether they still make sense.

Establishing New Goals

Finally, end the appraisal meeting by establishing new goals for the upcoming year. The process of goal setting is important, possibly as important as the goals themselves. Through setting professional goals with the employee, you and the employee discuss how achieving the goals will help the employee and the company. This gives the employee a sense of worth and a sense of how the employee can contribute to the company's success.

Although you may have come to the meeting prepared with ideas for goals, keep an open mind. The employee will also come prepared, and you may end up choosing the employee's goals over your own.

Writing Up the Requirements and Goals

Now that you have reassessed the requirements and chosen new goals, write them up according to the guidelines in Chapter 3. You can either attach them to the performance evaluation or write a separate memo to the employee's personnel file.

You are writing the requirements and goals in a document, not in stone. Throughout the appraisal period, you and the employee should be constantly reassessing whether these make sense given current conditions — within your department, within your company, and within the marketplace.

Test Your Knowledge

Questions

1. Conducting a performance appraisal is simply a matter of completing the evaluation form my company provides to me. ☐ True ☐ False

2. Because objective data does not contain opinions, it's the best data to use when evaluating an employee. ☐ True ☐ False

3. Whether the employee met the requirements and goals is only one of many questions to ask when drawing conclusions about an employee's performance. ☐ True ☐ False

4. When citing support for my conclusions about the employee's performance, I should choose only my best examples. ☐ True ☐ False

5. I should begin the meeting by setting an authoritative atmosphere so that the employee knows who's in charge. ☐ True ☐ False

6. It's not a good idea to ask the employee to do a self-evaluation because of the problems that might arise if the employee's opinion doesn't match my own. ☐ True ☐ False

7. The tone I use in the appraisal meeting is just as important as what I say. ☐ True ☐ False

8. Even if it is a routine chore for me, a performance evaluation is very important to my employees. ☐ True ☐ False

9. Performance evaluation meetings are a time for criticism, not praise. ☐ True ☐ False

10. One of the most important parts of the process comes at the end, when the employee and I reassess the job requirements and set new goals. ☐ True ☐ False

Answers

1. **False.** A year-end performance appraisal is a process during which you write up a formal performance evaluation and then meet with the employee to review the evaluation and discuss requirements and goals for the upcoming year. To write the evaluation, you gather information, draw conclusions, and then summarize your conclusions and supporting evidence in a document.

2. **False.** Objective data is quite useful, but it provides only part of the picture. You also need to review qualitative data, such as reports of significant events, a record of your own observations (for example, a performance log), interviews with other people (for example, customers, or other supervisors), and other documents (such as ticklers, kudos, and memos) to give you a full picture of an employee's performance.

3. **True.** You must also know why the employee did or did not meet the requirements and goals, and you must think about the impact the employee's performance had on the department and on the company as a whole. If the employee performed poorly, you must figure out what, if anything, you or others can do to help the employee improve in the future.

4. **True.** Use your best examples. There is no need to overwhelm the employee with every possible example as long as two or three demonstrate your point. If you conclude that the employee had exceptionally good or bad performance, however, you should provide more support.

5. **False.** The best atmosphere for the meeting is friendly, collaborative, and respectful. Together, the employee and you will go over the past year's performance and decide how the employee can do things better in the future. An authoritative tone may put the employee on the defensive, unable to hear your feedback and unable to give input.

6. **False.** Employee self-evaluation is a useful tool that puts the employee in the right frame of mind and engenders respect for the appraisal process. If the employee and you disagree in your evaluations, that's okay: Discussing the differences may help solve performance problems.

7. **True.** If you choose the right tone and the right words, you can ward off negative responses (such as defensiveness and anger) and maintain a productive meeting.

8. **True.** A year-end performance appraisal meeting may be the only time of the year when the employee gets your undivided time and attention to discuss how he or she is doing at work.

9. **False.** The performance evaluation is the place to talk about an employee's entire performance—both good and bad—over the appraisal period. This means that you should give praise if the employee has earned it and constructive criticism if necessary.

10. **True.** Although a big focus of this process is on past performance, the real benefit comes from determining what the employee can do going forward.

Performance Evaluation

Employee: _____

Job Title: _____

Appraiser: _____

Job Title: _____

Appraisal Period: _____

Requirements (ranked in order from most important to least important):

1. Requirement priority number _____

2. State the requirement: _____

_____

_____

3. Did the employee meet the requirement? _____

_____

_____

4. Explain: _____

_____

_____

_____

_____

5. Employee's comments: _____

_____

_____

_____

_____

_____

6. Appraisal meeting notes: _____

_____

_____

_____

_____

1. Requirement priority number _____

2. State the requirement: _____
   _____
   _____
   _____
   _____

3. Did the employee meet the requirement? _____
   _____
   _____
   _____
   _____

4. Explain: _____
   _____
   _____
   _____
   _____
   _____

5. Employee's comments: _____
   _____
   _____
   _____
   _____
   _____

6. Appraisal meeting notes: _____
   _____
   _____
   _____
   _____
   _____
   _____
   _____

Goals (ranked in order from most important to least important):

1. Goal priority number _____

2. State the goal: _____
_____
_____

3. Did the employee meet the goal? _____
_____
_____

4. Explain: _____
_____
_____
_____
_____
_____
_____

5. Employee's comments: _____
_____
_____
_____
_____
_____
_____
_____
_____

6. Appraisal meeting notes: _____
_____
_____
_____
_____
_____
_____
_____
_____
_____

1. Goal priority number ____
2. State the goal: _____
_____
_____

3. Did the employee meet the goal? _____
_____
_____

4. Explain: _____
_____
_____

5. Employee's comments: _____
_____
_____
_____
_____

6. Appraisal meeting notes: _____
_____
_____
_____
_____

Summary of any disciplinary problems:

_____
_____
_____
_____
_____
_____
_____
_____
_____

Appendix A

How to Use the Forms CD-ROM

The tear-out forms in Appendix B are included on a CD-ROM in the back of the book. This CD-ROM, which can be used with Windows computers, installs files that you use with software programs that are already installed on your computer. It is *not* a standalone software program. Please read this appendix and the README.TXT file included on the CD-ROM for instructions on using the Forms CD.

Note to Mac users: This CD-ROM and its files should also work on Macintosh computers. Please note, however, that Nolo cannot provide technical support for non-Windows users.

How to View the README File

If you do not know how to view the file README.TXT, insert the Forms CD-ROM into your computer's CD-ROM drive and follow these instructions:

- **Windows 2000, XP, and Vista:** (1) On your PC's desktop, double click the My Computer icon; (2) double click the icon for the CD-ROM drive into which the Forms CD-ROM was inserted; (3) double click the file README.TXT.
- **Macintosh:** (1) On your Mac desktop, double click the icon for the CD-ROM that you inserted; (2) double click the file README.TXT.

While the README file is open, print it out by using the Print command in the File menu.

Three different kinds of files are contained on the CD-ROM:

- Word processing (RTF) forms that you can open, complete, print, and save with your word processing program (see "Using the Word Processing Files to Create Documents," below),
- Forms (PDF) that can be viewed only with Adobe Reader (see "Using PDF Files to Print Out Forms," below). These forms are designed to be printed out and filled in by hand or with a typewriter, and
- MP3 audio files that you can listen to using your computer's media or MP3 player (see "Listening to the Audio Files," below)

See below for a list of forms, their file names, and their file formats.

Installing the Form Files Onto Your Computer

Before you can do anything with the files on the CD-ROM, you need to install them onto your hard disk. In accordance with U.S. copyright laws, remember that copies of the CD-ROM and its files are for your personal use only. The form files must be installed; installing the audio files, however, is optional.

Listening Without Installing

If you don't want to copy 16 MB of audio files to your hard disc, you can "play" the CD on your computer. For details, see "Playing the Audio Files Without Installing," below.

Insert the Forms CD and do the following.

Windows 2000, XP, and Vista Users

Follow the instructions that appear on the screen. (If nothing happens when you insert the Forms CD-ROM, then (1) double click the My Computer icon; (2) double click the icon for the CD-ROM drive into which the Forms CD-ROM was inserted; (3) double click the file WELCOME.EXE.)

By default, all the files are installed to the \Appraisal Resources folder in the \Program Files folder of your computer. A folder called "Appraisal Resources" is added to the "Programs" folder of the Start menu.

Macintosh Users

Step 1: If the "Appraisal Resources" window is not open, open it by double clicking the "Appraisal Resources" icon.

Step 2: Select the "Appraisal Resources" folder icon.

Step 3: Drag and drop the folder icon onto the icon of your hard disk.

Using the Word Processing Files to Create Documents

This section concerns the files for forms that can be opened and edited with your word processing program.

All word processing forms come in rich text format. These files have the extension ".RTF." For example, the form for the Form: Kudos to You discussed in Chapter 4 is on the file Kudos.rtf. All forms, their file names, and their file formats are listed below.

RTF files can be read by most recent word processing programs including all versions of MS Word for Windows and Macintosh, WordPad for Windows, and recent versions of WordPerfect for Windows and Macintosh.

To use a form from the CD to create your documents you must: (1) open a file in your word processor or text editor; (2) edit the form by filling in the required information; (3) print it out; (4) rename and save your revised file.

The following are general instructions. However, each word processor uses different commands to open, format, save, and print documents. Please read your word processor's manual for specific instructions on performing these tasks.

Do not call Nolo's technical support if you have questions on how to use your word processor or your computer.

Step 1: Opening a File

There are three ways to open the word processing files included on the CD-ROM after you have installed them onto your computer:

- Windows users can open a file by selecting its shortcut as follows: (1) Click the Windows "Start" button; (2) open the "Programs" folder; (3) open the "Appraisal Resources" subfolder; (4) open the "RTF" subfolder; (5) click the shortcut to the form you want to work with.
- Both Windows and Macintosh users can open a file directly by double clicking it. Use My Computer or Windows Explorer (Windows 2000, XP, or Vista) or the Finder (Macintosh) to go to the folder you installed or copied the CD-ROM's files to. Then, double click the specific file you want to open.

- You can also open a file from within your word processor. To do this, you must first start your word processor. Then, go to the File menu and choose the Open command. This opens a dialog box where you will tell the program (1) the type of file you want to open (*.RTF); and (2) the location and name of the file (you will need to navigate through the directory tree to get to the folder on your hard disk where the CD's files have been installed).

Where Are the Files Installed?

Windows Users: RTF files are installed by default to a folder named \Appraisal Resources\RTF in the \Program Files folder of your computer.

Macintosh Users: RTF files are located in the "RTF" folder within the "Appraisal Resources" folder.

Step 2: Editing Your Document

Fill in the appropriate information according to the instructions and sample agreements in the book. Underlines are used to indicate where you need to enter your information, frequently followed by instructions in brackets. Be sure to delete the underlines and instructions from your edited document. You will also want to make sure that any signature lines in your completed documents appear on a page with at least some text from the document itself.

Editing Forms That Have Optional or Alternative Text

Some of the forms have optional or alternate text:
- With optional text, you choose whether to include or exclude the given text.
- With alternative text, you select one alternative to include and exclude the other alternatives.

When editing these forms, we suggest you do the following.

Optional text

If you **don't want** to include optional text, just delete it from your document.

If you **do want** to include optional text, just leave it in your document.

In either case, delete the italicized instructions.

Alternative text

First delete all the alternatives that you do not want to include, then delete the italicized instructions.

Step 3: Printing Out the Document

Use your word processor's or text editor's "Print" command to print out your document.

Step 4: Saving Your Document

After filling in the form, use the "Save As" command to save and rename the file. Because all the files are "read-only," you will not be able to use the "Save" command. This is for your protection. *If you save the file without renaming it, the underlines that indicate where you need to enter your information will be lost and you will not be able to create a new document with this file without recopying the original file from the CD-ROM.*

Using PDF Files to Print Out Forms

Electronic copies of useful forms are included on the CD-ROM in Adobe Acrobat PDF format. You must have the Adobe Reader installed on your computer to use these forms. Adobe Reader is available for all types of Windows and Macintosh systems. If you don't already have this software, you can download it for free at www.adobe.com.

All forms, their file names, and their file formats are listed below.

These forms cannot be filled out using your computer. To create your document using these files, you must: (1) open the file; (2) print it out; (3) complete it by hand or typewriter.

Step 1: Opening PDF Files

PDF files, like the word processing files, can be opened one of three ways.

- Windows users can open a file by selecting its shortcut as follows: (1) Click the Windows "Start" button; (2) open the "Programs" folder; (3) open the "Appraisal Resources" subfolder, (4) open the "PDF" folder; (5) click the shortcut to the form you want to work with.

- Both Windows and Macintosh users can open a file directly by double clicking it. Use My Computer or Windows Explorer (Windows 2000, XP, or Vista) or the Finder (Macintosh) to go to the folder you created and copied the CD-ROM's files to. Then, double click the specific file you want to open.

- You can also open a PDF file from within Adobe Reader. To do this, you must first start Reader. Then, go to the File menu and choose the Open command. This opens a dialog box where you will tell the program the location and name of the file (you will need to navigate through the directory tree to get to the folder on your hard disk where the CD's files have been installed). If these directions are unclear, you will need to look through Adobe Reader's help—Nolo's technical support department will *not* be able to help you with the use of Adobe Reader.

Where Are the PDF Files Installed?

Windows Users: PDF files are installed by default to a folder named \Appraisal Resources\PDF in the \Program Files folder of your computer.

Macintosh Users: PDF files are located in the "PDF" folder within the "Appraisal Resources" folder.

Step 2: Printing PDF Files

Choose Print from the Adobe Reader File menu. This will open the Print dialog box. In the "Print Range" section of the Print dialog box, select the appropriate print range, then click OK.

Step 3: Filling In PDF Files

The PDF files cannot be filled out using your computer. To create your document using one of these files, you must first print it out (see Step 2, above), and then complete it by hand or typewriter.

Listening to the Audio Files

This section explains how to use your computer's media player to listen to the audio files. All audio files are in MP3 format. (Most computers come with a media player that plays MP3 files.) For example, "Interview with Amy DelPo" is on the file Interview-DelPo.mp3. At the end of this appendix, you'll see a list of the audio files and their file names.

You can listen to files that you have installed on your computer, or you can listen without having installed the files to your hard disk. (See "Playing the Audio Files Without Installing," below).

Please keep in mind that these are general instructions—because every media player is unique, these steps may not mirror the steps you need to follow to use your player. Please do not contact Nolo's technical support if you are having difficulty using your media player.

Listening to Audio Files You've Installed on Your Computer

There are two ways to listen to the audio files that you have installed on your computer.

- Windows users can open a file by selecting its shortcut as follows: (1) Click the Windows "Start" button, (2) open the "Programs" folder, (3) open the "Appraisal Resources" subfolder, (4) open the "Audio" subfolder; (5) click the shortcut to the audio segment you want to hear.
- Both Windows and Macintosh users can open a file directly by double clicking it. Use My Computer or Windows Explorer (Windows 2000, XP, or Vista) or the Finder (Macintosh) to go to the folder in which you installed or copied the CD-ROM's files. Then, double click the MP3 file you want to hear.

Where Are the Files Installed?

Windows Users: MP3 files are installed by default to a folder named \Appraisal Resources\Audio in the \Program Files folder of your computer.

Macintosh Users: MP3 files are located in the "Appraisal Audio" folder.

Playing the Audio Files Without Installing

If you don't want to copy 16 MB of audio files to your hard disk, you can "play" the CD on your computer. Here's how:

Window users

Step 1: Insert the Forms CD to view the "Welcome to Appraisal Resources CD" window. (If nothing happens when you insert the Forms CD-ROM, (1) double click the My Computer icon; (2) double click the icon for the CD-ROM drive into which the Forms CD-ROM was inserted; (3) double click the file WELCOME.EXE.)

Step 2: Click "Listen to Audio."

Mac users

Step 1: Insert the Forms CD. If the "Appraisal Resources CD" window does not open, open it by double clicking the "Appraisal Resources CD" icon.

Step 2: Open the "Appraisal Audio" folder by double clicking the "Appraisal Audio" icon.

Step 3: Double click the audio file you want to hear.

List of Files Included on the Forms CD-ROM

The following files are in rich text format (RTF).

Title	**File Name**
Form: Kudos to You	Kudos.rtf
Form: Performance Evaluation	Evaluation.rtf
Form: Performance Log	Log.rtf
Form: Tickler for You	Tickler.rtf

The following files are in Adobe Reader PDF format.

Title	**File Name**
Checklist: Agenda for the Year-End Appraisal Meeting	Agenda.pdf
Checklist: Assessing Performance	Assess.pdf
Checklist: Avoiding Legal Trouble	Avoid.pdf
Checklist: Common Performance Appraisal Errors	Errors.pdf
Checklist: Documenting Performance	Document.pdf
Checklist: Identifying Goals	Goals.pdf
Checklist: Identifying Job Requirements	Require.pdf
Checklist: Information to Gather for a Performance Appraisal	Gather.pdf
Checklist: Preparing an Employee for Goal Setting	Prepare.pdf
Checklist: Rules for Effective Discipline	Rules.pdf
Checklist: Writing Performance Objectives	Write.pdf

The following files are in MP3 format.

Title	**File Name**
Interview With Amy DelPo	Interview-DelPo.mp3
Interview With Margie Mader-Clark	Interview-Mader-Clark.mp3

Appendix B

Tear-Out Checklists and Forms

Checklists:

Avoiding Legal Trouble

Identifying Job Requirements

Preparing an Employee for Goal Setting

Identifying Goals

Writing Performance Objectives

Documenting Performance

Information to Gather for a Performance Appraisal

Assessing Performance

Common Performance Appraisal Errors

Agenda for the Year-End Appraisal Meeting

Forms:

Performance Log

Kudos to You

Tickler for You

Performance Evaluation

Checklist:
Avoiding Legal Trouble

As you put the finishing touches on a performance appraisal, review the following statements. If you cannot say any of them with certainty, then you may have stepped into a legal trap. In that case, reread the section of Chapter 2 that pertains to the issue.

In this performance evaluation:

☐ I do not make any predictions about the employee's future at this company.

☐ I do not promise the employee continued employment.

☐ I do not reassure the employee that his or her job is secure.

☐ I do not predict how likely it is that the employee will receive a promotion.

☐ I have not limited or softened my criticism of the employee's performance to be nice or to avoid conflict.

☐ I have not left out any issues because I don't want to confront the employee about them.

☐ I have not tried to spare the employee's feelings by ignoring or downplaying problems.

☐ I was able to thoroughly review this employee's performance, so the evaluation is comprehensive.

☐ If I am thinking that I may have to fire the employee someday, I have reflected the reasons behind such thoughts.

☐ I do not use slurs or potentially offensive language.

☐ I do not make any sexual comments.

☐ I do not make jokes.

☐ I do not say or imply anything that criticizes the employee for being different from others (for example, the employee "doesn't fit in") unless I have specifically related it to job performance.

- ☐ If the employee has one or more protected characteristics, I have not mentioned the characteristic(s).

- ☐ I have not based my evaluation on any stereotypes I might have about the employee based on the employee's protected characteristic(s).

- ☐ All of the feedback I have included is specific and related to the employee's job.

- ☐ If the employee has a physical or mental impairment, I have consulted with either human resources or the company's legal counsel before completing this evaluation.

- ☐ If the employee has complained about discrimination, harassment, or another violation of workplace law, or supported another employee's complaint, I have been very careful to document any negative feedback I have included. I have evaluated the employee fairly and have not given negative feedback just to get back at the employee for complaining.

- ☐ If I were questioned about anything I have included in this evaluation, I could support my statements with documents or other evidence.

Checklist:
Identifying Job Requirements

Here is a list of resources to consult when identifying job requirements:

- ☐ Your company's core values as evidenced in its strategic plan, mission statement, and values statements.

- ☐ The job description.

- ☐ Interviews with the employee who currently holds the job.

- ☐ Past evaluations for employees who held the position.

- ☐ Resumes of top performers in the position.

- ☐ Exit interviews with people who held the job.

- ☐ Interviews with coworkers, customers, and vendors who interact with the jobholder.

Checklist:
Preparing an Employee for Goal Setting

Before your goal-setting session with an employee (either in an initial meeting or at each year-end evaluation meeting), make sure that you:

☐ Provide a copy of your company's strategic plan and/or core values.

☐ If your company has made projections about the future that are relevant to the employee's job, provide those.

☐ Provide a current job description for the employee's position.

☐ For current employees, provide a copy of the employee's performance evaluation from the previous year.

☐ Ask the employee to make a list of professional development goals:

    ☐ What training would the employee like?

    ☐ What skills would the employee like to acquire or hone?

    ☐ What new tasks or responsibilities would the employee like to take on?

Checklist:
Identifying Goals

When identifying performance goals, make sure each one meets the following criteria:

- ☐ It is consistent with company goals.

- ☐ It is reasonable and realistic.

- ☐ It is challenging but within the employee's reach.

- ☐ It is specific.

- ☐ It is related to the employee's job.

- ☐ It is measurable or, if it cannot be measured, it is especially specific.

- ☐ If necessary, it has an action plan attached.

- ☐ It does not try to change the employee's personality.

- ☐ It is not based on assumptions or stereotypes.

- ☐ It does not promise the employee something now or in the future.

Checklist:
Writing Performance Objectives

When you write up a performance objective—be it a job requirement or a goal—make sure it meets these criteria:

- ☐ It is specific, not general.

- ☐ It describes what the employee should do, not who the employee should be.

- ☐ It contains concrete details.

- ☐ It uses active verbs, not passive verbs.

- ☐ If the requirement or goal is measurable, it describes how it will be measured.

- ☐ If appropriate, it gives a deadline for completion.

- ☐ Unless it is obvious, the objective describes how it relates to the job.

Checklist:
Documenting Performance

When you write a performance log entry, kudos, or a tickler, or send an email about performance, make sure it meets these criteria:

☐ It contains concrete and specific details—dates, times, places, names, numbers, and so on.

☐ It is accurate and doesn't exaggerate.

☐ It doesn't contain slurs or other inappropriate or derogatory terms.

☐ It doesn't contain language that could be construed as discriminatory or biased.

☐ It doesn't focus on personality issues.

☐ It focuses on behavior, performance, conduct, and productivity.

☐ It is complete.

☐ It contains job-related incidents only. It doesn't include entries about the employee's personal life or aspects of the employee that have nothing to do with the job.

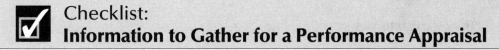

Checklist:
Information to Gather for a Performance Appraisal

As you prepare to write your performance appraisal, gather the following documents and records.

Objective Data:

- ☐ sales numbers
- ☐ earnings reports
- ☐ call records
- ☐ productivity reports
- ☐ deadline reports
- ☐ output and production records
- ☐ budget reports
- ☐ attendance records
- ☐ training or continuing education records
- ☐ time records

Critical Incidents:

- ☐ kudos
- ☐ ticklers
- ☐ customer complaints or compliments
- ☐ disciplinary notices
- ☐ personnel file

Personal Observations:

- ☐ performance log
- ☐ notes, emails, and/or phone messages

Third-Party Interviews:

- ☐ other managers
- ☐ clients/customers
- ☐ coworkers
- ☐ vendors

Other:

- ☐ work product
- ☐ current job description
- ☐ previous year's performance appraisal, including requirements and goals for the current year

Checklist:
Assessing Performance

Consider the following questions when assessing performance:

- ☐ Has the employee met this requirement or goal?
- ☐ Why or why not?
- ☐ How do I know this?
- ☐ What is the supporting evidence?
- ☐ What was the impact on the department? On the company?
- ☐ How can the employee do better?
- ☐ How can I do a better job of supporting the employee?
- ☐ How can the company do a better job of supporting the employee?

Consider the following possible reasons for poor performance:

- ☐ Did I give the employee adequate training?
- ☐ Does the employee have the skills necessary for the job?
- ☐ Does the employee understand what I expect?
- ☐ Have I provided the employee with adequate tools and resources?
- ☐ Are there any rules or systems in place that make it difficult for the employee to perform well?
- ☐ Has anything changed in the employee's work situation?
- ☐ Has anything happened in the employee's personal life that could be affecting his or her work?
- ☐ Has the employee developed a substance abuse or mental health problem?

Checklist:
Common Performance Appraisal Errors

After you have drawn conclusions about an employee's performance, ask yourself the following questions. If you can answer yes to any of them, then you've fallen prey to a common appraisal error—and you must rethink your conclusions.

☐ Have I rated the employee more highly than he or she deserves?

☐ Did I unfairly blame the employee for bad events or unfairly take credit (or give credit to someone else) for good events?

☐ Did I allow my first impressions to color what the employee did during this appraisal period?

☐ Did I allow one aspect of the employee's performance to dominate?

☐ Did I judge the employee more favorably because of our similarities?

☐ Did I judge the employee less favorably because of our differences?

☐ Did I gravitate to the middle to make this evaluation easier on myself?

☐ Did I ignore anything exceptionally good or bad about the employee's performance?

☐ Did I unfairly paint the employee as being either all good or all bad?

☐ Did I place too much weight on recent events?

☐ Have I made assumptions about or stereotyped the employee?

☐ Have I accurately described the employee's performance without fear of making the employee mad or of hurting the employee's feelings?

Checklist:
Agenda for the Year-End Appraisal Meeting

Although you should conduct the meeting in a way that feels natural and appropriate to you, here is a good sequence of events and topics to cover:

- ☐ Start with some introductory remarks.
- ☐ Give each other copies of your evaluation.
- ☐ Go through each requirement and goal.
- ☐ Reassess the job requirements.
- ☐ Choose goals for the coming year.
- ☐ End the meeting on a positive note.

Performance Log
CONFIDENTIAL

Employee Name: _____

Employee Title: _____

Date	Incident	Kudos/ Tickler/ Oral Reminder/ Written Warning (see personnel file)

Kudos to You

To: _____

From: _____

Cc: _____

Date: _____

_____

_____

_____

_____

_____

_____

_____

_____

_____

_____

_____

_____

_____

_____

_____

_____

_____

_____

_____

_____

_____

_____

We are only as good as our employees. Thanks for your efforts!

Tickler for You

To: _____

From: _____

Cc: _____

Date: _____

_____

_____

_____

_____

_____

_____

_____

_____

_____

_____

_____

_____

_____

_____

_____

_____

_____

_____

_____

_____

_____

_____

_____

_____

I know you can get back on track!

Performance Evaluation

Employee: _____

Job Title: _____

Appraiser: _____

Job Title: _____

Appraisal Period: _____

Requirements (ranked in order from most important to least important):

1. Requirement priority number _____

2. State the requirement: _____
   _____
   _____

3. Did the employee meet the requirement? _____
   _____
   _____

4. Explain: _____
   _____
   _____
   _____
   _____

5. Employee's comments: _____
   _____
   _____
   _____
   _____

6. Appraisal meeting notes: _____
   _____
   _____

1. Requirement priority number _____

2. State the requirement: _____
   _____
   _____

3. Did the employee meet the requirement? _____
   _____
   _____

4. Explain: _____
   _____
   _____
   _____
   _____

5. Employee's comments: _____
   _____
   _____
   _____
   _____
   _____
   _____

6. Appraisal meeting notes: _____
   _____
   _____
   _____
   _____
   _____
   _____
   _____
   _____

Goals (ranked in order from most important to least important):

1. Goal priority number _____

2. State the goal: _____
   _____
   _____

3. Did the employee meet the goal? _____
   _____
   _____

4. Explain: _____
   _____
   _____
   _____
   _____
   _____

5. Employee's comments: _____
   _____
   _____
   _____
   _____
   _____
   _____
   _____

6. Appraisal meeting notes: _____
   _____
   _____
   _____
   _____
   _____
   _____
   _____

1. Goal priority number _____

2. State the goal: _____
   _____

3. Did the employee meet the goal? _____
   _____
   _____

4. Explain: _____
   _____
   _____

5. Employee's comments: _____
   _____
   _____
   _____

6. Appraisal meeting notes: _____
   _____
   _____
   _____

Summary of any disciplinary problems:

_____
_____
_____
_____
_____
_____
_____
_____
_____
_____
_____
_____
_____
_____
_____
_____

Appendix C

State and Federal Laws Prohibiting Discrimination

Federal Fair Employment Laws

Title VII of the Civil Rights Act of 1964 (commonly referred to as "Title VII")

Legal citation:

42 U.S.C. §§ 2000e and following

Covered employers:

- private employers with 15 or more employees
- state governments and their agencies
- local governments and their agencies
- the federal government and its agencies
- employment agencies
- labor unions

Prohibited conduct:

Title VII prohibits employers from discriminating against applicants and employees on the basis of race or color, religion, sex, pregnancy, childbirth, and national origin (including membership in a Native American tribe).

Title VII also prohibits harassment based on any of the protected characteristics listed above.

Title VII also prohibits an employer from retaliating against someone who asserts his or her rights under Title VII.

Title VII's prohibition against discrimination applies to all terms, conditions, and privileges of employment.

Enforcing agency:

The U.S. Equal Employment Opportunity Commission

The Age Discrimination in Employment Act (commonly referred to as the "ADEA")

Legal citation:

29 U.S.C. §§ 621-634

Covered employers:

- private employers with 20 or more employees
- the federal government and its agencies (note that employees of state governments and their agencies cannot sue for damages under ADEA)
- local governments and their agencies
- employment agencies
- labor unions

Prohibited conduct:

The ADEA prohibits discrimination against employees who are age 40 or older. The ADEA also prohibits harassment of those employees based on their age. The ADEA also prohibits employers from retaliating against employees who assert their rights under the ADEA.

The ADEA's prohibition against discrimination applies to all terms, conditions, and privileges of employment.

Enforcing agency:

The U.S. Equal Employment Opportunity Commission

The Equal Pay Act

Legal citation:

29 U.S.C. § 206(d)

Covered employers:

- virtually all private employers (regardless of the number of employees)
- the federal government and its agencies
- state governments and their agencies
- local governments and their agencies
- employment agencies
- labor unions

Prohibited conduct:

Employers cannot pay different wages to men and women who do substantially equal work.

Enforcing agency:

The U.S. Equal Employment Opportunity Commission

The Immigration Reform and Control Act of 1986 (commonly referred to as the "IRCA")

Legal citation:

8 U.S.C. § 1324

Covered employers:

- private employers with four or more employees
- the federal government and its agencies
- state governments and their agencies
- local governments and their agencies
- employment agencies
- labor unions

Prohibited conduct:

The IRCA prohibits employers from discriminating against applicants or employees on the basis of their citizenship or national origin. The IRCA's prohibition against discrimination applies to all terms, conditions, and privileges of employment.

The IRCA also makes it illegal for employers to knowingly hire or retain in employment people who are not authorized to work in the United States.

It also requires employers to keep records that verify that their employees are authorized to work in the United States.

The Americans With Disabilities Act (commonly referred to as the "ADA")

Legal citation:

42 U.S.C. §§ 12101–12213

Covered employers:

- private employers with 15 or more employees
- the federal government and its agencies (but employees of state governments and their agencies cannot sue for damages under ADEA)
- local governments and their agencies
- employment agencies
- labor unions

Prohibited conduct:

The ADA prohibits employers from discriminating against a person who has a disability or who is perceived to have a disability in any aspect of employment.

The ADA also prohibits employers from refusing to hire someone or discriminating against someone because that person is related to or associates with someone with a disability.

The ADA also prohibits harassment of the people described above.

The ADA prohibits retaliation against people who assert their rights under the ADA.

Enforcing agencies:

The U.S. Equal Employment Opportunity Commission and the U.S. Department of Justice

State Laws Prohibiting Discrimination in Employment

State	Law applies to employers with	Age	Ancestry or national origin	Disability	AIDS/HIV	Gender	Marital status	Pregnancy, childbirth, and related medical conditions	Race or color	Religion or creed	Sexual orientation	Genetic testing information	Additional protected categories
			Private employers may not make employment decisions based on										
Alabama Ala. Code §§ 25-1-20, 25-1-21	20 or more employees	40 and older											
Alaska Alaska Stat. §§ 18.80.220, 47.30.865	One or more employees	40 and older	✓	Physical and mental	✓	✓	✓ (Includes changes in status)	✓ Parenthood	✓	✓			Mental illness
Arizona Ariz. Rev. Stat. §§ 41-1461, 41-1463	15 or more employees	40 and older	✓	Physical	✓	✓			✓	✓		✓	
Arkansas Ark. Code Ann. §§ 16-123-102, 16-123-107 11-4-601, 11-5-403	9 or more employees		✓	Physical and mental		✓		✓	✓	✓		✓[1]	
California Cal. Gov't. Code §§ 12920, 12941; Cal. Lab. Code § 1101	5 or more employees	40 and older	✓	Physical and mental	✓	✓	✓	✓	✓	✓	✓	✓	• Gender identity • Medical condition • Political activities or affiliations
Colorado Colo. Rev. Stat. §§ 24-34-301, 24-34-401, 24-34-402, 27-10-115	One or more employers	40 to 70	✓	Physical, mental, and learning	✓	✓			✓	✓	✓		• Lawful conduct outside of work • Mental illness
Connecticut Conn. Gen. Stat. Ann. §§ 46a-51, 46a-60, 46a-81	3 or more employees	40 and older	✓	Present or past physical, mental, or learning	✓	✓	✓	✓	✓	✓		✓	Mental retardation
Delaware Del. Code Ann. tit. 19, §§ 710, 711	4 or more employees	40 and older	✓	Physical or mental	✓	✓	✓	✓	✓	✓		✓	

[1] Employees covered by FLSA

State Laws Prohibiting Discrimination in Employment (continued)

State	Law applies to employers with	Age	Ancestry or national origin	Disability	AIDS/HIV	Gender	Marital status	Pregnancy, childbirth, and related medical conditions	Race or color	Religion or creed	Sexual orientation	Genetic testing information	Additional protected categories
District of Columbia D.C. Code Ann. §§ 2-1401.01, 2-1401.02, 7-1703.03	One or more employers	18 and older	✓	Physical or mental	✓	✓	✓ (Includes domestic partnership)	✓ Parenthood	✓	✓	✓	✓	• Enrollment in vocational, professional, or college education • Family duties • Source of income • Place of residence or business • Personal appearance • Political affiliation • Smoker • Any reason other than individual merit
Florida Fla. Stat. Ann. §§ 760.01, 760.02, 760.10, 760.50, 448.075	15 or more employees		✓	"Handicap"	✓	✓	✓		✓	✓			Sickle cell trait
Georgia Ga. Code Ann. §§ 34-6A-1, and following, 34-5-1, 34-5-2	15 or more employees (disability) 10 or more employees (gender)			Physical or mental		✓[2]							
Hawaii Haw. Rev. Stat. § 378-1, 378-2	One or more employees		✓	Physical or mental	✓	✓	✓	✓ Breastfeeding	✓	✓	✓	✓	Arrest and court record (unless there is a conviction directly related to job)
Idaho Idaho Code §§ 67-5902, 67-5909	5 or more employees	40 and older	✓	Physical or mental		✓		✓	✓	✓			
Illinois 775 Ill. Comp. Stat. §§ 5/1-102, 5/1-103, 5/2-101, 5/2-102; Ill. Admin. Code tit. 56, § 5210.110	15 or more employees One or more employees (disability)	40 and older	✓	Physical or mental	✓	✓	✓	✓	✓	✓	✓		• Citizen status • Military status • Unfavorable military discharge

[2] Wage discrimination only

State Laws Prohibiting Discrimination in Employment (continued)

State	Law applies to employers with	Age	Ancestry or national origin	Disability	AIDS/HIV	Gender	Marital status	Pregnancy, childbirth, and related medical conditions	Race or color	Religion or creed	Sexual orientation	Genetic testing information	Additional protected categories
Indiana Ind. Code Ann. §§ 22-9-1-2, 22-9-3, 22-9-2-1, 22-9-2-2	6 or more employees	40 to 70	✓	Physical or mental (15 or more employees)		✓			✓	✓			
Iowa Iowa Code § 216.2, 216.6	4 or more employees	18 or older	✓	Physical or mental	✓	✓		✓	✓	✓		✓	
Kansas Kan. Stat. Ann. §§ 44-1001, 44-1002, 44-1112, 44-1113, 44-1125, 44-1126, 65-6002(e)	4 or more employees	18 or older	✓	Physical or mental	✓	✓			✓	✓		✓	Military status
Kentucky Ky. Rev. Stat. Ann. §§ 344.030, 344.040, 207.130, 207.150, 342.197	8 or more employees	40 or older	✓	Physical	✓	✓			✓	✓			• Smoker or nonsmoker • Occupational pneumoconiosis with no respiratory impairment resulting from exposure to coal dust
Louisiana La. Rev. Stat. Ann. §§ 23:301 to 23:352	20 or more employees	40 or older	✓	Physical or mental		✓		✓ (Applies to employers with 25 or more employees)	✓	✓		✓	Sickle cell trait
Maine Me. Rev. Stat. Ann. tit. 5, §§ 4552, 4553, 4571	One or more employees		✓	Physical or mental		✓		✓	✓	✓	✓	✓	• Past workers' compensation claim • Past whistle-blowing
Maryland Md. Code 1957 Art. 49B, §§ 15, 16	15 or more employees		✓	Physical or mental		✓	✓	✓	✓	✓	✓	✓	
Massachusetts Mass. Gen. Laws ch. 151B, §§ 1, 4	6 or more employees	40 or older	✓	Physical or mental	✓	✓	✓		✓	✓	✓	✓	• Military service • Arrests

State Laws Prohibiting Discrimination in Employment (continued)

State	Law applies to employers with	Age	Ancestry or national origin	Disability	AIDS/HIV	Gender	Marital status	Pregnancy, childbirth, and related medical conditions	Race or color	Religion or creed	Sexual orientation	Genetic testing information	Additional protected categories
Michigan Mich. Comp. Laws §§ 37.1201, 37.1202, 37.2201, 37.2202, 37.1103	One or more employees		✓	Physical or mental	✓	✓	✓	✓	✓	✓		✓	• Height or weight • Arrest record
Minnesota Minn. Stat. Ann. §§ 363A.03, 363A.08, 181.974	One or more employees	18 or older	✓	Physical or mental	✓	✓	✓	✓	✓	✓	✓	✓	• Gender identity • Member of local commission • Perceived sexual orientation • Receiving public assistance
Mississippi Miss. Code Ann. §§ 33-1-15													• Military status (all employers) • No other protected categories unless employer receives public funding
Missouri Mo. Rev. Stat. §§ 213.010, 213.055, 191.665, 375.1306	6 or more employees	40 to 70	✓	Physical or mental	✓	✓		✓	✓	✓		✓	
Montana Mont. Code Ann. §§ 49-2-101, 49-2-303	One or more employees		✓	Physical or mental		✓	✓	✓	✓	✓			
Nebraska Neb. Rev. Stat. §§ 48-1101, 48-1102, 48-1001 to 48-1002, 20-168	15 or more employees	40 to 70[3]	✓	Physical or mental	✓	✓	✓	✓	✓	✓		✓	
Nevada Nev. Rev. Stat. Ann. §§ 613.310 and following	15 or more employees	40 or older	✓	Physical or mental		✓		✓	✓	✓	✓	✓	• Lawful use of any product when not at work • Use of service animal

[3] Employers with 25 or more employees

State Laws Prohibiting Discrimination in Employment (continued)

State	Law applies to employers with	Age	Ancestry or national origin	Disability	AIDS/HIV	Gender	Marital status	Pregnancy, childbirth, and related medical conditions	Race or color	Religion or creed	Sexual orientation	Genetic testing information	Additional protected categories
New Hampshire N.H. Rev. Stat. Ann. §§ 354-A2, 354-A6, 354-A7, 141-H:3	6 or more employees	✓	✓	Physical or mental		✓	✓	✓	✓	✓	✓	✓	
New Jersey N.J. Stat. Ann. §§ 10:5-5 to 10:5-12, 34:6B-1	One or more employees	18 to 70	✓	Past or present physical or mental	✓	✓	✓ (Includes domestic partner)	✓	✓	✓	✓	✓	• Predisposing genetic characteristics • Military service or status • Smoker or nonsmoker
New Mexico N.M. Stat. Ann. § 28-1-2, 28-1-7	4 or more employees	40 or older[4]	✓	Physical or mental		✓	✓ (Applies to employers with 50 or more employees)	✓	✓	✓	✓[5]		• Gender identity (employers with 15 or more employees) • Serious medical condition
New York N.Y. Exec. Law § 292, 296; N.Y. Lab. Law § 201-d	4 or more employees	18 and over	✓	Physical or mental	✓	✓	✓	✓	✓	✓	✓	✓	• Lawful use of any product when not at work • Military status • Observance of Sabbath • Political activities
North Carolina N.C. Gen. Stat. §§ 143-422.2, 95-28.1, 127B-11, 130A-148, 168A-3, 168A-5	15 or more employees	✓	✓	Physical or mental	✓	✓			✓	✓		✓	• Lawful use of any product when not at work • Sickle cell trait
North Dakota N.D. Cent. Code §§ 14-02.4-02, 14-02.4-03, 34-01-17	One or more employees	40 or older	✓	Physical or mental		✓	✓	✓	✓	✓			• Lawful conduct outside of work • Receiving public assistance

[4] Employers with 20 or more employees
[5] Employers with 15 or more employees

State Laws Prohibiting Discrimination in Employment (continued)

State	Law applies to employers with	Age	Ancestry or national origin	Disability	AIDS/HIV	Gender	Marital status	Pregnancy, childbirth, and related medical conditions	Race or color	Religion or creed	Sexual orientation	Genetic testing information	Additional protected categories
Ohio Ohio Rev. Code Ann. §§ 4111.17, 4112.01, 4112.02	4 or more employees	40 or older	✓	Physical, mental, or learning		✓		✓	✓	✓			
Oklahoma Okla. Stat. Ann. tit. 25, §§ 1301, 1302; tit. 36, § 3614.2; tit. 40, § 500; tit. 44, § 208	15 or more employees	40 or older	✓	Physical or mental		✓			✓	✓		✓	• Military service • Smoker or nonsmoker
Oregon Or. Rev. Stat. §§ 659A.001 and following, 659A.303	One or more employees	18 or older	✓	Physical or mental	✓	✓		✓	✓	✓	✓		
Pennsylvania 43 Pa. Cons. Stat. Ann. § 954-955	4 or more employees	40 to 70	✓	Physical or mental		✓		✓	✓	✓			• Familial status • GED rather than high school diploma • Use of guide or service animal
Rhode Island R.I. Gen. Laws §§ 28-6-18, 28-5-6, 28-5-7, 23-6-22, 12-28-10	4 or more employees One or more employees (gender-based wage discrimination)	40 or older	✓	Physical or mental	✓	✓		✓	✓	✓	✓	✓	• Domestic abuse victim • Gender identity or expression
South Carolina S.C. Code Ann. §§ 1-13-30, 1-13-80	15 or more employees	40 or older	✓	Physical or mental		✓		✓	✓	✓			
South Dakota S.D. Codified Laws Ann. §§ 20-13-1, 20-13-10, 60-12-15, 60-2-20, 62-1-17	One or more employees		✓	Physical, mental, and learning		✓			✓	✓		✓	Preexisting injury

State Laws Prohibiting Discrimination in Employment (continued)

State	Law applies to employers with	Age	Ancestry or national origin	Disability	AIDS/HIV	Gender	Marital status	Pregnancy, childbirth, and related medical conditions	Race or color	Religion or creed	Sexual orientation	Genetic testing information	Additional protected categories
Tennessee Tenn. Code Ann. §§ 4-21-102, 4-21-401 and following; 8-50-103, 50-2-201, 50-2-202	8 or more employees One or more employees (gender-based wage discrimi-nation)	40 or older	✓	Physical or mental		✓			✓	✓			
Texas Tex. Lab. Code Ann. §§ 21.002, 21.052, 21.101, 21.402	15 or more employees	40 or older	✓	Physical or mental		✓		✓	✓	✓		✓	
Utah Utah Code Ann. § 34A-5-102, 34-5-106	15 or more employees	40 or older	✓	Follows federal law	✓	✓		✓	✓	✓			
Vermont Vt. Stat. Ann. tit. 21, § 495, 495d; tit. 18, § 9333	One or more employees	18 or older	✓	Physical or mental	✓	✓			✓	✓	✓	✓	Place of birth
Virginia Va. Code Ann. §§ 2.2-3900, 40.1-28.6, 51.5-41	Law applies to all employers	✓	✓	Physical or mental		✓	✓	✓	✓	✓		✓	Use of a service animal
Washington Wash. Rev. Code Ann. §§ 38.40.110, 49.60.040, 49.60.172, 49.60.180, 49.12.175, 49.44.090; Wash. Admin. Code 162-30-020	8 or more employees One or more employees (gender-based wage discrimi-nation)	40 or older	✓	Physical, mental, or sensory	✓	✓	✓	✓	✓	✓		✓	• Hepatitis C infection • Member of state militia • Use of a trained guide dog

State Laws Prohibiting Discrimination in Employment (continued)

State	Law applies to employers with	Age	Ancestry or national origin	Disability	AIDS/HIV	Gender	Marital status	Pregnancy, childbirth, and related medical conditions	Race or color	Religion or creed	Sexual orientation	Genetic testing information	Additional protected categories
West Virginia W.Va. Code §§ 5-11-3, 5-11-9, 21-5B-1, 21-5B-3, 21-3-19	12 or more employees One or more employees (gender-based wage discrimination)	40 or older	✓	Physical or mental	✓	✓			✓	✓			Smoking away from work
Wisconsin Wis. Stat. Ann. §§ 111.32 and following	One or more employees	40 or older	✓	Physical or mental	✓	✓	✓	✓	✓	✓	✓	✓	• Arrest or conviction • Lawful use of any product when not at work • Military service or status
Wyoming Wyo. Stat. §§ 27-9-102, 27-9-105, 19-11-104	2 or more employees	40 or older	✓	Not specified		✓			✓	✓			• Military service or status • Smoking off duty

Current as of February 2006

Index

R

S

CATALOG

...more from Nolo

BUSINESS	PRICE	CODE
Business Buyout Agreements (Book w/CD-ROM)	$49.99	BSAG
The CA Nonprofit Corporation Kit (Binder w/CD-ROM)	$69.99	CNP
California Workers' Comp: How to Take Charge When You're Injured on the Job	$34.99	WORK
The Complete Guide to Buying a Business (Book w/CD-ROM)	$24.99	BUYBU
The Complete Guide to Selling a Business (Book w/CD-ROM)	$24.99	SELBU
Consultant & Independent Contractor Agreements (Book w/CD-ROM)	$29.99	CICA
The Corporate Records Handbook (Book w/CD-ROM)	$69.99	CORMI
Create Your Own Employee Handbook (Book w/CD-ROM)	$49.99	EMHA
Dealing With Problem Employees	$44.99	PROBM
Deduct It! Lower Your Small Business Taxes	$34.99	DEDU
Effective Fundraising for Nonprofits	$24.99	EFFN
The Employer's Legal Handbook	$39.99	EMPL
Essential Guide to Federal Employment Laws	$39.99	FEMP
Form a Partnership (Book W/CD-ROM)	$39.99	PART
Form Your Own Limited Liability Company (Book w/CD-ROM)	$44.99	LIAB
Home Business Tax Deductions: Keep What You Earn	$34.99	DEHB
How to Form a Nonprofit Corporation (Book w/CD-ROM)—National Edition	$49.99	NNP
How to Form a Nonprofit Corporation in California (Book w/CD-ROM)	$49.99	NON
How to Form Your Own California Corporation (Binder w/CD-ROM)	$59.99	CACI
How to Form Your Own California Corporation (Book w/CD-ROM)	$34.99	CCOR
How to Write a Business Plan (Book w/CD-ROM)	$34.99	SBS
Incorporate Your Business (Book w/CD-ROM)	$49.99	NIBS
Investors in Your Backyard (Book w/CD-ROM)	$24.99	FINBUS
The Job Description Handbook	$29.99	JOB

Prices subject to change.

	PRICE	CODE
Legal Guide for Starting & Running a Small Business	$34.99	RUNS
Legal Forms for Starting & Running a Small Business (Book w/CD-ROM)	$29.99	RUNSF
Lower Taxes in 7 Easy Steps	$16.99	LTAX
LLC or Corporation?	$24.99	CHENT
The Manager's Legal Handbook	$39.99	ELBA
Marketing Without Advertising	$20.00	MWAD
Music Law (Book w/CD-ROM)	$39.99	ML
Negotiate the Best Lease for Your Business	$24.99	LESP
Nolo's Guide to Social Security Disability (Book w/CD-ROM)	$29.99	QSS
Nolo's Quick LLC	$29.99	LLCQ
The Performance Appraisal Handbook	$29.99	PERF
The Progressive Discipline Handbook (Book w/CD-ROM)	$34.99	SDHB
The Small Business Start-up Kit (Book w/CD-ROM)	$24.99	SMBU
The Small Business Start-up Kit for California (Book w/CD-ROM)	$24.99	OPEN
Starting & Running a Successful Newsletter or Magazine	$29.99	MAG
Tax Deductions for Professionals	$34.99	DEPO
Tax Savvy for Small Business	$36.99	SAVVY
Whoops! I'm in Business	$19.99	WHOO
Working for Yourself: Law & Taxes for Independent Contractors, Freelancers & Consultants	$39.99	WAGE
Working With Independent Contractors (Book w/CD-ROM)	$29.99	HICI
Your Crafts Business: A Legal Guide (Book w/CD-ROM)	$26.99	VART
Your Limited Liability Company: An Operating Manual (Book w/CD-ROM)	$49.99	LOP
Your Rights in the Workplace	$29.99	YRW

CONSUMER

	PRICE	CODE
How to Win Your Personal Injury Claim	$29.99	PICL
Nolo's Encyclopedia of Everyday Law	$29.99	EVL
Nolo's Guide to California Law	$24.99	CLAW
Your Little Legal Companion (Hardcover)	$9.95	ANNI

	PRICE	CODE

ESTATE PLANNING & PROBATE

	PRICE	CODE
8 Ways to Avoid Probate	$19.99	PRAV
Estate Planning Basics	$21.99	ESPN
The Executor's Guide: Settling a Loved One's Estate or Trust	$34.99	EXEC
How to Probate an Estate in California	$49.99	PAE
Make Your Own Living Trust (Book w/CD-ROM)	$39.99	LITR
Nolo's Simple Will Book (Book w/CD-ROM)	$36.99	SWIL
Plan Your Estate	$44.99	NEST
Quick & Legal Will Book (Book w/CD-ROM)	$19.99	QUIC
Special Needs Trust: Protect Your Child's Financial Future (Book w/CD-ROM)	$34.99	SPNT

FAMILY MATTERS

	PRICE	CODE
Always Dad	$16.99	DIFA
Building a Parenting Agreement That Works	$24.99	CUST
The Complete IEP Guide	$34.99	IEP
Divorce & Money: How to Make the Best Financial Decisions During Divorce	$34.99	DIMO
Divorce Without Court	$29.99	DWCT
Do Your Own California Adoption: Nolo's Guide for Stepparents & Domestic Partners (Book w/CD-ROM)	$34.99	ADOP
Every Dog's Legal Guide: A Must-Have for Your Owner	$19.99	DOG
Get a Life: You Don't Need a Million to Retire Well	$24.99	LIFE
The Guardianship Book for California	$34.99	GB
A Judge's Guide to Divorce (Book w/CD-ROM)	$24.99	JDIV
A Legal Guide for Lesbian and Gay Couples	$34.99	LG
Living Together: A Legal Guide (Book w/CD-ROM)	$34.99	LTK
Nolo's Essential Guide to Divorce	$24.99	NODV
Nolo's IEP Guide: Learning Disabilities	$29.99	IELD
Parent Savvy	$19.99	PRNT
Prenuptial Agreements: How to Write a Fair & Lasting Contract (Book w/CD-ROM)	$34.99	PNUP
Work Less, Live More	$17.99	RECL

	PRICE	CODE

GOING TO COURT

	PRICE	CODE
Beat Your Ticket: Go To Court & Win! (National Edition)	$21.99	BEYT
The Criminal Law Handbook: Know Your Rights, Survive the System	$39.99	KYR
Everybody's Guide to Small Claims Court (National Edition)	$29.99	NSCC
Everybody's Guide to Small Claims Court in California	$29.99	CSCC
Fight Your Ticket & Win in California	$29.99	FYT
How to Change Your Name in California	$29.99	NAME
Nolo's Deposition Handbook	$29.99	DEP
Represent Yourself in Court: How to Prepare & Try a Winning Case	$39.99	RYC
Win Your Lawsuit: A Judge's Guide to Representing Yourself in California Superior Court	$29.99	SLWY

HOMEOWNERS, LANDLORDS & TENANTS

	PRICE	CODE
Buying a Second Home (Book w/CD-ROM)	$24.99	SCND
California Tenants' Rights	$27.99	CTEN
Deeds for California Real Estate	$24.99	DEED
Every Landlord's Legal Guide (National Edition, Book w/CD-ROM)	$44.99	ELLI
Every Landlord's Guide to Finding Great Tenants (Book w/CD-ROM)	$19.99	FIND
Every Landlord's Tax Deduction Guide	$34.99	DELL
Every Tenant's Legal Guide	$29.99	EVTEN
For Sale by Owner in California	$29.99	FSBO
How to Buy a House in California	$29.99	BHCA
The California Landlord's Law Book: Rights & Responsibilities (Book w/CD-ROM)	$44.99	LBRT
The California Landlord's Law Book: Evictions (Book w/CD-ROM)	$44.99	LBEV
Leases & Rental Agreements	$29.99	LEAR
Neighbor Law: Fences, Trees, Boundaries & Noise	$26.99	NEI
Renters' Rights (National Edition)	$24.99	RENT

IMMIGRATION

	PRICE	CODE
Becoming A U.S. Citizen: A Guide to the Law, Exam and Interview	$24.99	USCIT
Fiancé & Marriage Visas (Book w/CD-ROM)	$34.99	IMAR

	PRICE	CODE
How to Get a Green Card	$29.99	GRN
Student & Tourist Visas	$29.99	ISTU
U.S. Immigration Made Easy	$39.99	IMEZ

MONEY MATTERS

101 Law Forms for Personal Use (Book w/CD-ROM)	$29.99	SPOT
Chapter 13 Bankruptcy: Repay Your Debts	$39.99	CHB
Credit Repair (Book w/CD-ROM)	$24.99	CREP
How to File for Chapter 7 Bankruptcy	$29.99	HFB
IRAs, 401(k)s & Other Retirement Plans: Taking Your Money Out	$34.99	RET
Solve Your Money Troubles	$19.99	MT
Stand Up to the IRS	$29.99	SIRS

PATENTS AND COPYRIGHTS

All I Need is Money: How to Finance Your Invention	$19.99	FINA
The Copyright Handbook: How to Protect and Use Written Works (Book w/CD-ROM)	$39.99	COHA
Copyright Your Software (Book w/CD-ROM)	$34.95	CYS
Getting Permission: How to License & Clear Copyrighted Materials Online & Off (Book w/CD-ROM)	$34.99	RIPER
How to Make Patent Drawings	$29.99	DRAW
The Inventor's Notebook	$24.99	INOT
Nolo's Patents for Beginners	$24.99	QPAT
Patent, Copyright & Trademark	$39.99	PCTM
Patent It Yourself	$49.99	PAT
Patent Pending in 24 Hours	$34.99	PEND
Patenting Art & Entertainment: New Strategies for Protecting Creative Ideas	$39.99	PATAE
Profit from Your Idea (Book w/CD-ROM)	$34.99	LICE
The Public Domain	$34.99	PUBL
Trademark: Legal Care for Your Business and Product Name	$39.99	TRD

	PRICE	CODE
Web and Software Development: A Legal Guide (Book w/CD-ROM)	$44.99	SFT
What Every Inventor Needs to Know About Business & Taxes (Book w/CD-ROM)	$21.99	ILAX

RESEARCH & REFERENCE

Legal Research: How to Find & Understand the Law	$39.99	LRES

SENIORS

Long-Term Care: How to Plan & Pay for It	$19.99	ELD
Social Security, Medicare & Goverment Pensions	$29.99	SOA

SOFTWARE

Call or check our website at www.nolo.com for special discounts on Software!

Incorporator Pro	$89.99	STNC1
LLC Maker—Windows	$89.95	LLP1
Patent Pending Now!	$199.99	PP1
PatentEase—Windows	$349.00	PEAS
Personal RecordKeeper 5.0 CD—Windows	$59.95	RKD5
Quicken Legal Business Pro 2007—Windows	$109.99	SBQB7
Quicken WillMaker Plus 2007—Windows	$79.99	WQP7

Special Upgrade Offer

Save 35% on the latest edition of your Nolo book

Because laws and legal procedures change often, we update our books regularly. To help keep you up-to-date, we are extending this special upgrade offer. Cut out and mail the title portion of the cover of your old Nolo book and we'll give you 35% off the retail price of the New Edition of that book when you purchase directly from Nolo. This offer is to individuals only. Prices and offer subject to change without notice.

Order Form

Name				Our "No-Hassle" Guarantee

Our "No-Hassle" Guarantee

Return anything you buy directly from Nolo for any reason and we'll cheerfully refund your purchase price. No ifs, ands or buts.

☐ Check here if you do not wish to receive mailings from other companies

Name

Address

City

State, Zip

Daytime Phone

E-mail

Item Code	Quantity	Item	Unit Price	Total Price

Method of payment

☐ Check   ☐ VISA

☐ American Express

☐ MasterCard

☐ Discover Card

Subtotal	
Add your local sales tax (California only)	
Shipping: RUSH $12, Basic $9 (See below)	
"I bought 3, ship it to me FREE!" (Ground shipping only)	
TOTAL	

Account Number

Expiration Date

Signature

Shipping and Handling

Rush Delivery—Only $12

We'll ship any order to any street address in the U.S. by UPS 2nd Day Air* for only $12!

* Order by noon Pacific Time and get your order in 2 business days. Orders placed after noon Pacific Time will arrive in 3 business days. P.O. boxes and S.F. Bay Area use basic shipping. Alaska and Hawaii use 2nd Day Air or Priority Mail.

Basic Shipping—$9

Use for P.O. Boxes, Northern California and Ground Service.

Allow 1-2 weeks for delivery.

U.S. addresses only.

For faster service, use your credit card and our toll-free numbers

Call our customer service group Monday thru Friday 7am to 7pm PST

 Phone
1-800-728-3555

 Fax
1-800-645-0895

 Mail
Nolo
950 Parker St.
Berkeley, CA 94710

Order 24 hours a day @ www.nolo.com

Get the Latest in the Law

1. Nolo's Legal Updater
We'll send you an email whenever a new edition of your book is published! Sign up at **www.nolo.com/legalupdater**.

2. Updates at Nolo.com
Check **www.nolo.com/update** to find recent changes in the law that affect the current edition of your book.

3. Nolo Customer Service
To make sure that this edition of the book is the most recent one, call us at **800-728-3555** and ask one of our friendly customer service representatives (7:00 am to 6:00 pm PST, weekdays only). Or find out at **www.nolo.com**.

4. Complete the Registration & Comment Card ...
... and we'll do the work for you! Just indicate your preferences below:

Registration & Comment Card

NAME _____ DATE _____

ADDRESS _____

CITY _____ STATE _____ ZIP _____

PHONE _____ EMAIL _____

COMMENTS _____

WAS THIS BOOK EASY TO USE?   (VERY EASY)   5   4   3   2   1   (VERY DIFFICULT)

☐ Yes, you can quote me in future Nolo promotional materials. *Please include phone number above.*

☐ Yes, send me **Nolo's Legal Updater** via email when a new edition of this book is available.

Yes, I want to sign up for the following email newsletters:

  ☐ **NoloBriefs** (monthly)
  ☐ **Nolo's Special Offer** (monthly)
  ☐ **Nolo's BizBriefs** (monthly)
  ☐ **Every Landlord's Quarterly** (four times a year)

☐ Yes, you can give my contact info to carefully selected partners whose products may be of interest to me.

NOLO

PERF 2.0

Nolo
950 Parker Street
Berkeley, CA 94710-9867
www.nolo.com

- -

YOUR LEGAL COMPANION